tough minds
tender hearts

For Margaret,
Catherine, Rebecca
and Anna

tough minds
tender hearts

HOLDING
truth & love
TOGETHER

JONATHAN LAMB

inter-varsity press

INTER-VARSITY PRESS

38 De Montfort Street, Leicester LE1 7GP, England

First published 1997

British Library Cataloguing in Publication Data
A catalogue record for this book is available from the British Library.

ISBN 0–85111–183–1

Set in Garamond No. 3 and Bodoni

Typeset in Great Britain by Parker Typesetting Service, Leicester

Printed and bound in Great Britain by
The Guernsey Press Co. Ltd., Guernsey, Channel Islands

*Inter-Varsity Press is the book-publishing division of the Universities and Colleges
Christian Fellowship (formerly the Inter-Varsity Fellowship), a student movement
linking Christian Unions in universities and colleges throughout the United Kingdom
and the Republic of Ireland, and a member movement of the International Fellowship of
Evangelical Students. For information about local and national activities write to
UCCF, 38 De Montfort Street, Leicester LE1 7GP.*

Contents

Preface   7

1. *Better together*   9

2. *This is our God*   15

3. *Truth in a confused world*   31

4. *Truth in action*   51

5. *Love in a broken world*   65

6. *Christian unity*   89

7. *Christian differences*   103

8. *Christian co-operation*   125

9. *Christian growth*   143

Preface

Being British, I am often told by my friends in other parts of Europe that I should know a good deal about compromise. I am not too sure whether to take it as a compliment. For the word 'compromise', like the word 'balanced', tends to get a bad press. Such positions – or such people – are bland and grey!

To be a balanced Christian doesn't seem to be that appealing – unless of course, we understand the concept very differently. Balance is not holding a middle position between two apparently irreconcilable extremes. It is holding *both* extreme positions at the same time. This is much more the picture we are given in the Bible, and means we live our lives with passionate and colourful conviction rather than the monotones of carefully negotiated compromise.

The concern of this book is that the two great Christian themes of truth and love are frequently seen as opposite poles rather than intimate friends. But held together they provide the true focus for the Christian life, the deepest expression of the Christian faith, the most powerful dynamic that the world has ever seen. For they arise from the heart of God's nature, are expressed in the life and ministry of God's Son, and are to be embodied and demonstrated in God's people.

It has taken some while to express these thoughts in written form, and I need to record my gratitude to a succession of patient IVP editors who have encouraged me forward in the task, most particularly Stephanie Heald. Almost every day I see my need for the Spirit's help in expressing both the conviction and the compassion which are essential to a properly balanced Christian life, and I hope that what follows will encourage churches, student groups and individual Christians to be biblical extremists in their commitment to the truth and love that are found in God himself. I am more than ever convinced that today's church needs truth to set the course and love to fill the sails.

I would also like to record my thanks to students and staff in IFES who have frequently challenged my thinking and, particularly, to express gratitude to my wife Margaret who, despite the frequent pressures associated with our life together in Christian service, has displayed the qualities about which I have tried to write.

Jonathan Lamb
Oxford, November 1996

Better together

Dragging her out of bed and through the cold streets, the hostile crowd was delighted with its catch. She stood lonely and condemned, surrounded by her male accusers. They viewed her with contempt – a woman of the street who could be bought for the price of a meal. Now, shivering in the courtyard, she could serve their purposes and then be discarded. Her self-righteous accusers smirked: 'Teacher, this woman was caught in the act of adultery. In the law, Moses commanded us to stone such a woman. Now what do you say?'

They were not too bothered about the woman, or about the nature of her indiscretion. What mattered was Jesus' reaction to the question, set as a carefully baited trap. To support the stoning would not only bring him into conflict with the Roman authorities but effectively destroy his credibility as a man of the people. But to reject the punishment would signal his rejection of the Jewish law.

In one of the most memorable dramatic moments in the gospels, Jesus wrote with his finger on the dirt floor. 'If any one of you is without sin, let him be the first to throw a stone at her' (Jn. 8:7). As her accusers slowly turned away one by one, the woman was left alone with Jesus. 'Neither do I condemn you . . . Go and leave your life of sin' (Jn. 8:11).

Had Jesus gone soft? Was he ignoring failure and glossing over sin? By no means. In fact, his response was powerful and incisive, exposing the truth about both the adulteress and the religious leaders. Jesus was not dismissing moral order. He spoke of the need of repentance and forgiveness, but he also provided the resources for fresh moral resolve and for a new direction. 'Go and sin no more.' The truth would set her free, as Jesus explained in the verses which follow. Mercy and grace would demand a new life, lived according to the standards of God's law and empowered by his truth.

In this one encounter, Jesus demonstrated why he was introduced by the gospel writer as the man 'full of grace and truth' (Jn. 1:14). Unlike the scribes and Pharisees, who displayed the arrogance of religion at its worst, his words and actions demonstrated compassion, not cynicism; forgiveness, not condemnation.

Grace and truth combine in Jesus to make the gospel deeply transforming. It is this which makes the Christian good news so powerful and attractive. Together they stand for compassion and conviction; together they reach heart as well as mind. Frequently they are kept apart, and our purpose in this book is to demonstrate why their marriage is so essential to dynamic Christian living.

Truth without love

I sometimes meet thoughtful but disillusioned Christians whose encounter with Christian leaders has left them feeling like the condemned woman dragged to the temple. Christianity for them has been hard and unbending. Judging it by the exclusive, arrogant, condemnatory attitudes of its exponents, they have understandably found it repellent. They have become disillusioned, not because of their inability to believe in God, but because of their distaste for those who speak in his name. Plenty of truth, perhaps, but little grace.

Quite frequently, when speaking at churches in Britain, I am taken aside for a quiet conversation with a church member who is struggling with other Christians within the fellowship. The most common reason for division in our churches is not the disagreement itself (whether doctrinal, strategic or temperamental), but our inability to handle differences with a firm combination of truth and love. Either we are reluctant to confront one another, or we ruthlessly expose failure without the gentleness which grace demands. The same must be said of pastoral ministry and our care for one another. Broken and wounded people sometimes leave the church because they have been told the truth about their fractured lives but have not been surrounded by love.

We also need truth and love to combine in our Christian proclamation and our partnership with others. Sometimes I am embarrassed by the tone and the style of those who insist they are 'standing for the truth'. I confess it is not uncommon for me, as a fellow evangelical committed to the truth of the gospel, to feel some shame at the outbursts of some of those who believe as I do. They seem to lack Christian grace, they fail to respect others who bear the name 'Christian', and they appear to disobey the truth by the way they try to defend it.

As we shall see, we cannot dodge the challenge of standing up for the truth. Paul's letters give us many warnings about the danger of diluting the gospel. We cannot take the easy way out and avoid the confrontation of proclaiming God's truth in a hostile world. For love demands that we take truth seriously. Our compassion for those around us will compel us to pass on the only message of truth that can meet their deepest needs. But 'conviction with compassion' is the model for Christian proclamation.

Love without truth

A well-known media caricature gives us another distorted version of the Christian faith. An eccentric, scruffily dressed bishop tells us that belief in the reality of the gospel events is not critical; what matters is identifying the love of God in whatever religion it may be found. Tolerance, openness, flexibility – these are today's religious priorities. This position is comfortable and soft. Just as arrogant and judgmental religion produces disillusioned

Christians, this version inevitably has the same effect: people lose their way in an ineffectual, anaemic faith, which lacks the radical transforming power that Jesus displayed.

We shall turn in chapters 3 and 4 to our understanding of truth. We imagine that truth is a cold, academic set of propositions. But to see it as it is – a powerful and life-giving force that can shape our lives and our communities – will radically alter our commitment to the Bible and to the ministry of the Spirit of truth. Doing the truth, living the truth and embodying the truth are what matters. This is what sharpens the impact and the integrity of our Christian witness.

Love is not separate from truth in Christian discipleship. It is not a sugar-coated, sentimental idea which allows us to do as we please. It is the framework within which truth operates, the atmosphere in which truth thrives. In chapter 5 we shall examine the priority of love, and we shall see that, just as truth in action leads to love, so obedient love will reflect and empower the truth. Truth sets the course; love fills the sails.

Christian reality

I know many young people around Europe who have come to living faith through an encounter with Jesus Christ in the gospels. Reading and debating the gospel stories, they have become drawn towards this immensely attractive figure, so unlike the religious stereotypes they have encountered elsewhere. Here is someone who mixes with the outcast and the socially unaccept-able, and who rejects religious humbug and hypocrisy; a man whose concern is to make people whole rather than to tear them apart; a man with convictions and with compassion.

He is Jesus, the incarnate Word of grace and truth, and it is this combination of qualities that is central to his character and that reflects the nature of God himself. Such a powerful and life-transforming combination should influence every aspect of our Christian life and community.

Some years ago, I met a young woman whose first encounter with Christians was not unlike meeting the accusing crowd of religious bigots who had dragged the woman before Jesus. She was visually handicapped and, abandoned by her parents, had been brought up in a children's home. She had been sexually abused, and resorted to drug-taking. The first Christians she met told her that she was going to hell because she had had an abortion. It was some years later, through the care of Christians involved with Torch Trust for the Blind, that she was finally able to overcome the sense of rejection she had initially felt from Christians. She experienced their compassion and their gentle correction. She came to see the grace and truth that are in Jesus.

If we are committed to live Christ's life, how is it that so frequently we fail to act as God's truth and love demand? Why do we get it so terribly wrong?

Cultural trends

To begin with, our understanding of truth and love is often shaped by the prevailing attitudes within the culture of our day, rather than by a firm understanding of biblical teaching. And because of this, the two concepts are frequently kept apart. We imagine that we can be either truthful or loving, but we cannot easily be both at the same time. Behind this assumption lies an inadequate understanding and experience of God. We have all heard it said: 'I can accept the God of the New Testament. He's the God of love. But don't give me the God of the Old Testament – all that wrathful vengeance and needless killing.' Our God of love is soft and sentimental; our God of truth is a spoilsport, a tyrant and a judge.

Moreover, our age is deeply cynical about the very concepts of both truth and love. Whether it is in the counsellor's surgery, the politician's manifesto, the DJ's studio, the editor's newsdesk, the children's classroom or even the bishop's palace, we meet distortions of truth and love at every turn. It does not take long before the cultural drift begins subtly to shape Christian thinking too. These trends appeal to our sinfulness and pride and our inbuilt tendency to think of ourselves rather than others. We fail to allow our new life in Christ to govern our reactions and our relationships.

But the Bible affirms throughout its pages that in God the

qualities of truth and love find their purest and most powerful expression. He is the source of both, and they are the essence of his nature, as we shall see in the next chapter. It is this partnership which shapes our understanding of his work in Christ, and his continuing actions towards us and a needy world. It moves our hearts in worship as we see his grace and truth focused in the cross; it helps us to perceive what motivates his actions of judgment; and it will help us face his discipline with a sense of gratitude. In turn, the marriage of conviction and compassion will shape the way Christians live together, work together and even disagree together.

In each of these ways we need to restore a proper understanding and integration of these twin qualities, found at the heart of God's nature, of the gospel, and of all true Christian living. 'There seems so often to be love without truth,' observes Michael Harper, 'and truth without love. Their divorce is a tragedy, their marriage a blessing beyond description.'[1]

Such a marriage reflects the nature of the God who is both Light and Love, and provides the direction and power which we so desperately need in our lives, our churches and our societies. And so this is where we shall begin – with the God who, in Christ, is described as 'full of grace and truth'.

Notes

1. Michael Harper, *The Love Affair* (Hodder and Stoughton, 1982), p. 40.

This is our God

> What comes into our minds when we think about God is the
> most important thing about us. *(A. W. Tozer)*

A distorted view of God is sure to lead to a distorted Christian life.
To see him only as tyrant and judge is to live our lives in fear. To see
him as soft and sentimental is to live our lives without resolve. But
knowing the true and living God will provide the foundations and
the motivation for a life which genuinely reflects his nature.

Let me begin by illustrating some of the misconceptions about
God which are common in our society.

In the woodlands north of Budapest, seated by a camp fire, Sara
held a letter in her hands. She was a deeply thoughtful Christian
student, committed to Christ and to sharing the gospel with her
fellow Hungarians. A non-Christian friend had written to her. He
had shared her church background in the past, but could not
share her Christian commitment.

She translated for me: 'I could not consider myself a sinner
from birth, for all the terrible thunder of an angry God. I find the
idea of worshipping a bloodthirsty, avenging, punishing Christian God repulsive.'

Many people brought up with some association with the
church harbour a similar suspicion about God. He is a God to be

feared, a distant and cruel tyrant. Another letter, published in our local newspaper, expressed how many people feel:

> Jesus was said to have died on the cross in agony to save humanity. I do not want salvation at such a price; I want nothing to do with a God who demands pain and suffering in order to be appeased. Man himself is the strongest evidence either of a malevolent force or of a God aloof from and indifferent to the affairs of this world, if indeed God exists at all. If there were a God both benevolent and omnipotent, he could have arranged things a whole lot better.

The challenge for my Hungarian friend is one that all Christians share. How do we communicate to those around us that the God of the Bible, the God of this universe, is the living God of grace and truth, whose heart is full of compassion towards them and towards all he has made?

Even within the church, many people do not have a rounded biblical view of God's character. In his description of the problem of nominal Christianity, Eddie Gibbs identifies several causes of the drift away from living faith. One of them is that the word of God has been proclaimed in a cold, abrasive and judgmental manner. Frustrated and angry preachers, as he puts it, are prone to play the role of an austere prophet, making stern pronouncements of judgment, and reinforcing the distorted view of God which too many churchgoers hold.

> Those who have sat and squirmed under such ministry have in reality rejected a caricature of the gospel and thereby missed out on the fundamental message of a God who so loved the world that he sent his only Son, not to condemn the world, but that the world might be saved through him.[1]

As we shall see in a moment, even those dark passages of Scripture which describe God's judgment and vengeance need to be seen within the context of God's overall purposes of love for his creation. But the caricature of the angry God is prevalent in the minds of many.

Another distortion – of a very different kind – comes from the neo-paganism of broad New Age thinking. God can be found in everyone. He is not the God of judgment, but the God of potential, growth and healing power. As we fulfill our potential, we are told, we become God. Shirley MacLaine is probably the best-known exponent of such popular New Age thinking. 'If you see God as the energy within – the New Testament God – you'll be better off than seeing him as a vengeful Old Testament God, and you'll respond to life in the same way.'[2] And there is a common misconception. He is the god who makes no demands upon us, a god fashioned according to our own desires. To believe in such a god means we can live according to our own preferences.

In the light of so many distorted impressions of the nature and character of God, it is vital that we gain a true biblical perspective, both for our own well-being as Christian disciples, and for the effectiveness of our Christian proclamation. In this book we shall focus on the themes of his love and his truth. We shall see how they are fully expressed in God, and how, in turn, they determine the shape of our Christian living and profoundly influence our worship, prayer, preaching and ministry.

Separating what in God is joined

Any human attempt to describe God is bound to be limited or inadequate. But one sure way of creating distortion is to separate one of God's attributes from the others, or even to set it against them.

This happens when, for instance, God's love is isolated from his other attributes – his righteousness, truthfulness or holiness. Writing on the 'God above' and the 'God with us', Dick France comments:

> Our danger is not in running to extremes – we cannot outrun the extent of either the holiness or the love of God – but in running to one extreme and forgetting the other. The correct balance in biblical theology is seldom the golden mean, the innocuous compromise, but the taking into our system of two

concepts so dynamic and so opposite that they must be seen to threaten to tear apart the hand that holds them.[3]

Don Carson, too, has expressed the point helpfully:

> It is possible to set up a polarisation such that his stern justice swamps his love and his forbearance, or the reverse; it is possible so to stress his sovereignty that we fall into mechanistic fatalism, or so to emphasize his personal relationships that we sacrifice his sovereignty. A substantial part of responsible biblical theology is learning how to tie complementary truths together.[4]

Moses was a man who realized that without God he could achieve nothing. Through his dependence on God, he understood more and more about God's character. After the failure and rebellion of the exodus story, and the monumental disaster of the golden calf, Moses longed for the certainty that God's presence would continue with his people. But more than that, he yearned for the enjoyment of a closer experience of God and of his glory.

His bold request is recorded in Exodus 33:18: 'Now show me your glory.' It was a request to see God as he is. It indicated the depth of this man's passion for God. Even though he is described as having an intimate relationship with the Lord, Moses was asking for the impossible. God is God, and no mortal can see his glory in its fullness. The Lord replied: 'You cannot see my face, for no-one may see me and live' (Ex. 33:20).

In fact, God gave him something better still. In a profound revelation of his nature, the Lord passed in front of Moses, proclaiming,

> The LORD, the LORD, the compassionate and gracious God, slow to anger, abounding in love and faithfulness, maintaining love to thousands, and forgiving wickedness, rebellion and sin. Yet he does not leave the guilty unpunished; he punishes the children and their children for the sin of the fathers to the third and fourth generation. *(Ex. 34:6–7)*

After all the experiences that Moses and the people had passed through, including personal and corporate failure of extraordinary dimensions, here was a revelation of the merciful and gracious God who would forgive where there was genuine repentance. We might think that if God is love, he cannot at the same time be the holy God who in righteous anger acts in judgment. But the revelation of God's glory which Moses witnessed demonstrates how the Lord's attributes are held together. This revelation of a righteous God can be something of a shock to those who hold to a kind of Santa Claus theology, imagining their God of love to be incapable of a strong word, and characterized only by benevolent softness. They misunderstand the nature of true love. In the Old Testament, God's wrath and justice are not incompatible with his love. There is no tension between them, since justice is an expression of his love. His discipline of individuals and of his own people expressed not only his justice, but also the stern love which a good father shows to his children, a love which wants to see his children change for the better.

It is vital that we relate God's love to his righteousness. By separating them, love becomes sloppy and sentimental, and righteousness becomes legalistic and harsh. Both belong at the heart of God's nature. To see how this is so, we shall look at three important biblical couplets. Each phrase is used by the biblical writers to demonstrate how the qualities of truth and love operate together in God's nature and his actions. The first is the frequent Old Testament pairing of God's 'steadfast love' and 'faithfulness'. The second speaks of Jesus, full of 'grace and truth'. The third is John's description of the heart of God's character: he is both Love and Light.

My reason for emphasizing each is deeply practical. He is the God we worship, the God we trust, the God who will guide us. Our lives as disciples and as congregations will be shaped decisively by our understanding of who he is.

God's commitment

In the pregnant statement of Exodus 34:6–7, two words stand out as typical of the covenant relationship between God and his people: steadfast love (*ḥeseḏ*) and faithfulness (*ᵉmeṯ*). Together they represent a statement of God's complete solidarity with us.

The first, *ḥeseḏ*, is one of the most important words for 'love' in the Old Testament, and expresses an idea which is deeply rooted in Hebrew religion. The distinct tone of the word implies relationship and indicates a deep, lasting affection. It is often used in the context of the special relationship between God and his people. It is 'love strengthened by loyalty'.

The second word, *ᵉmeṯ*, comes from the same root as 'Amen'. It emphasizes that which is established or unshakeable. It is one of the words for 'truth' found in the Old Testament. Unlike the capricious pagan gods, Yahweh is completely consistent and faithful to his promises. He is unchanging in his truth.

Place the two together and we have the most powerful yet moving declaration of God's nature found throughout the Old Testament. Many of the psalms celebrate that partnership in a wonderfully joyful way, and we should allow the truth of these songs to sink into our hearts. There are three practical results of knowing God's love and truth: we are secure; we are never beyond his reach; and we shall never be abandoned.

We are secure

The God of *ḥeseḏ* and *ᵉmeṯ* guarantees to protect his people. These are not abstract ideas, but describe God's active care for us. 'May your love and your truth always protect me' (Ps. 40:11). The combination is important for God's people because the foundation of trust is an awareness of God's absolute commitment to us (steadfast love) coupled with his absolute reliability (his truth or faithfulness). They are both completely dependable.

I once spoke with a young Danish Christian who faced the challenging task of leading an IFES Team in Tbilisi, Georgia. The country was passing through the upheaval experienced by many Soviet successor states: economic and social instability, political turmoil, mafia activity and civil strife. He described how he felt, serving the Lord in this new situation: 'There is no adventure; I have few possessions; there is much uncertainty. But I have the Lord. That is enough.' Christians under pressure know

God to be a living reality, whose love and faithfulness surround them and protect them. There can be no greater confidence or security for the Christian believer this side of heaven.

These two qualities take on an even more personal expression in David's appeal for guidance in Psalm 25. His song expresses his trust in the Lord, and deals with various sources of stress in his life – the pressure of enemies, the burden of guilt, and the longing to discover God's ways. The psalm demonstrates that God has good purposes for us, founded on his truth and love.

> Guide me in your *truth* and teach me,
>   for you are God my Saviour,
>   and my hope is in you all day long.
> Remember, O LORD, your great *mercy* and *love*,
>   for they are from of old . . .
> All the ways of the LORD are *loving* and *faithful*
>   for those who keep the demands of his covenant.
>
> (Ps. 25:5–6, 10)

Learning to trust someone takes time. It grows out of our knowledge of his or her character. Not long ago I had my first experience of abseiling. As I hung over a cliff on the west coast of Scotland – not much of a drop, but quite enough when going down backwards – I learnt a number of lessons, but one particularly important one: you must learn to trust. You have to trust the rope and the person at the top doing the belaying. I was willing to go over the top because I knew that my friend was holding the ropes. He had a sense of humour, but he would not go so far as to let me drop. Despite the emotional trauma, I am still here to tell the tale.

We trust people who are *trustworthy*, and that means we know their character. Whatever lay ahead of David, and however God led him, he was sure that God could be trusted. And so for us: the more we come to know God's steadfast love and faithfulness, the more we shall trust him. Since God's reliability is absolute, our trust in him can be exclusive. He is the safest guide in the universe.

We are never beyond his reach

The psalmists acknowledge that God's love and truth extend throughout his entire creation to the farthest reaches of heaven and earth. No-one is beyond the scope of his steadfast love.

> For the word of the LORD is right and true;
>   He is *faithful* in all he does.
> The LORD loves righteousness and justice;
>   the earth is full of his *unfailing love*.
>
> *(Ps. 33:4–5)*

> Your *love*, O LORD, reaches to the heavens,
>   your *faithfulness* to the skies.
>
> *(Ps. 36:5)*

'The whole world is full of God's grace and faithfulness, reaching up to the uttermost parts of the infinite heaven and its inaccessible cloud layers,' comments Artur Weiser on the latter passage.[5] He suggests that the song alludes to the Exodus passage we have looked at, with Moses standing on top of the mountain when the Lord's glory was revealed.

The infinite extent of God's love and truth carries two implications for us: one pastoral, the other missiological.

First, we are never beyond the reach of God's love and care. Although it is sometimes hard to trust him in a world so tainted by evil, God's faithfulness surrounds us, his commitment to his children can never be shaken, and his control of this world can never be successfully challenged.

Much of my time is spent working alongside small Christian groups which feel themselves to be under pressure. In many countries, true believers make up less than 1% of the population. Where they seek to witness to the truth with sensitivity and boldness, they are usually inviting mockery, rejection and isolation. It is humbling and deeply moving to sit in their prayer meetings and see their trust in the Lord. They understand the confidence of the psalmists: God's love and truth are unshakeable, whatever their circumstances and whatever remote corner of the globe they inhabit. They are never beyond God's reach.

Secondly, the poets and prophets of the Old Testament understood that because of God's nature of love and truth, his commitment extends to the whole of creation. His redemptive purposes are for every nation and every individual. One of the great motivating forces in our Christian mission is therefore that God's steadfast love and faithfulness are at the heart of his purposes for our world.

We shall never be abandoned

The Old Testament writers used the couplet of love and truth to stress that his commitment is eternal. Despite our failure, he refuses to abandon us. He never stops loving his wayward children.

This is expressed in moving terms by the sorrowful poet who wrote in the shadow of the fall of Jerusalem.

> The steadfast love of the LORD never ceases,
>   his mercies never come to an end . . .
> For men are not cast off
>   by the LORD for ever.
> Though he brings grief, he will show compassion,
>   so great is his unfailing love.

(La. 3:22 {RSV}, 31–32)

To come to understand and experience such steadfast love, even in moments of weakness and failure, is to enjoy one of the greatest privileges of God's children. William McConnell, the Deputy Governor of the Maze Prison in Northern Ireland, wrote these words shortly before he was assassinated a few years ago: 'I have committed my life, my talents, work and action to Almighty God, in the sure and certain knowledge that, however slight my hold on him may have been, his promises are sure and his hold on me complete.' McConnell had come to understand that because of God's love and truth, we who trust him are safe both in time and in eternity.

We are secure, we are never beyond his reach, and we shall never be abandoned. These fundamental convictions arise from understanding who God is. For the Old Testament writers, this marriage of truth and love was of the essence of God's nature, and a cause for deep thanksgiving and praise. It expressed the covenant relationship of God with his people (Ho. 2:19–20), and was a sure promise of mercy and faithfulness extending from one generation to the next. Although these affirmations were given to the people of God in the Old Testament, the theme has enormous relevance to the contemporary needs of everyone around us.

I recently met a Polish man at London's Heathrow Airport. We were both travelling to Warsaw; he was returning to visit his elderly mother after having been away from his country for some fourteen years. He described his life as a pilot for a Japanese airline, with his 'home' in Australia. Discovering that I had travelled to Poland frequently over the years, he quizzed me about the country, the changes, and the mood of young people. And then, with remarkable honesty, he told me, 'I have no idea who I am or where I belong.' His lostness was not to do with living in Australia, flying for the Japanese, and originating from Poland. It was a much more deep-set crisis of orientation, personal identity and security. His situation has often come to my mind in talking with today's younger generation. For there are in the hearts and minds of so many people a fundamental uncertainty and insecurity; they are orphans in the universe.

To such a generation the message of the gospel is supremely relevant. The God whom we have come to know through faith in Christ is the one to whom we belong. He is our home and our destiny. His love and faithfulness reach out to all men and women, irrespective of their culture or creed. In a world of insecurity, in a lonely and bewildering universe, the absolute reliability of God's steadfast love and truth remains as the foundation certainty of our lives.

Just as these two qualities are held together in the Godhead, so in turn God's people are to reflect them. That is what a covenant relationship is all about. In the Old Testament it was frequently at this point that they failed. In a remarkable passage, the Lord expresses his profound disappointment:

Hear the word of the LORD, O people of Israel;
  for the Lord has a controversy with the inhabitants of
    the land.
There is no faithfulness [^{ve}met] or kindness [$hesed$],
  and no knowledge of God in the land.

(Ho. 4:1, RSV)

Knowing God's character should lead to corresponding conduct. He looks to us to play our part:

Let love and faithfulness never leave you;
  bind them around your neck,
  write them on the tablet of your heart.

(Pr. 3:3)

God's clear sign

The American comedian and film director, Woody Allen, once quipped that he found it hard to believe in God. 'If only God would give me some clear sign — like placing a large deposit in my name in a Swiss bank account.' But the gospel writers leave no doubt that God has already given us the clearest of signs. He has given us his Son.

In a passage pointing us back to Exodus 34 and Moses' appeal to see God's glory, John tells us how he saw God's glory revealed in Jesus. In the prologue to his gospel, he twice describes Jesus in a phrase which is plainly the equivalent of the Old Testament couplet of love and faithfulness we have been looking at. Once again the two words relate to the revelation of God, this time in Jesus himself, who was full of 'grace and truth'.

The Word became flesh and made his dwelling among us. We have seen his glory, the glory of the One and Only, who came from the Father, full of grace and truth. (Jn. 1:14)

From the fulness of his grace we have all received one blessing after another. For the law was given through Moses; grace and truth came through Jesus Christ. (Jn. 1:16–17)

Just as God 'lived among' his people in the wilderness (in the tabernacle and the tent of meeting, Ex. 25:8; 33:7), so the Word has come to live among us: he has 'pitched his tent among us' (Jn. 1:14, literally). Now in an intimate and personal way, God has revealed himself to us. 'We have seen his glory, the glory of the One and Only' – nothing less than God's glory.

As we have seen, God revealed his glory to Moses on Mount Sinai, demonstrating his love and truth. Now, declares John, in Jesus Christ those same qualities are expressed to everyone who turns in faith to him. Moses was told that the compassionate Lord is '*abounding* in love and faithfulness [truth]' (Ex. 34:6); John speaks of grace and truth being revealed in all their *fullness* in Jesus. By his words and actions, Jesus perfectly expressed the partnership of truth and love which is the essence of the Godhead.

John goes further. Just as Jesus was 'full of grace and truth', so we, his people, have come to benefit from that same divine fullness. Just as we have received God's grace and truth, so we are to demonstrate them to others.

All of God's actions towards us are on the basis of that same grace and truth. Under the law of Moses, both grace and truth were set forth. The law revealed God's truth, and the sacrificial system expressed his mercy. But in Jesus Christ they are brought together. In flesh and blood he revealed what God's truth is like; on the cross, he revealed what God's love is like. In Jesus Christ, grace and truth have reached their completion and perfection and, with John, we can rejoice that 'from the fulness of his grace we have all received one blessing after another'. That is why knowing him is what Christianity is all about. He has not abandoned God's law; rather, he embodies God's truth. He does not represent an impossible standard; rather, through his love he has opened the way for us to share his nature. In him truth and love are perfectly represented.[6]

As a child I heard a preacher's story of a woman from London's East End who had very little to live on. One day a charitable organization hired a minibus and took her and her friends out of the grey and impoverished housing estate for a day by the sea. One of the volunteers saw the woman standing on the shoreline, gazing at the sea with tears in her eyes. Worried that she might not be enjoying the trip, the volunteer asked her why she was crying.

'It's lovely to see something there's so much of,' she replied.

This is what John is describing. While his prologue has provided theologians with much food for thought, these verses are not academic. Jesus brings us the fullness of grace and truth, and the overwhelming assurance of God's steadfast love and faithfulness that will never run dry. He completely fulfils God's purposes in showing us the heart of God, and leading us into that very same fullness.

This is the centre-point of the Christian faith: knowing Jesus Christ means knowing and experiencing the greatest treasures to be found in the universe. I feel I am only paddling in the shallows. But 'it's lovely to see something there's so much of'. From that fullness we receive one blessing after another.

God's character

John frequently stresses the partnership of love and truth. In his letters he emphasizes that these two attributes are at the heart of God's character. He uses two simple expressions to highlight this. In the clearest biblical statement of God's nature, John tells us that 'God is love' (1 Jn. 4:8). And to speak of God's truth, he explains that 'God is light; in him there is no darkness at all' (1 Jn. 1:5). Together these affirmations describe God's essence – the heart of his being – and provide us with another simple couplet which sums up his nature and actions towards us. He is Love and Light.

Light is an important metaphor throughout Scripture, and particularly in John's writings. Light symbolizes revelation. Light is truth, and darkness is either ignorance or error. The Old Testament frequently uses the idea of illumination linked to the concept of God's self-revelation or to his word. 'For these commands are a lamp, this teaching is a light' (Pr. 6:23). Light as a source of illumination and guidance, then, lies behind John's idea of 'walking in the light' as a metaphor for true Christian living.

Light also symbolizes God's righteousness and purity. Isaiah records how the people of Judah called 'evil good and good evil'; they 'put darkness for light and light for darkness' (Is. 5:20).

John brings together both ideas, intellectual and moral, in the way he uses light and darkness in his gospel. Frequently light depicts the revelation of God's truth (Jn. 1:4–5, 9; 8:12). Jesus' statement in 3:21 clearly demonstrates the link between belief in the truth and proper moral behaviour: 'Whoever lives by the truth comes into the light, so that it may be seen plainly that what he has done has been done through God.'

John thus shows us that truth is a partner of love. For how is the truth to be seen? How is the light to be demonstrated? To walk in the light will mean a twofold commitment: to practise the truth, revealed through Christ and the apostles (1 Jn. 1:5–7); and to love one another.

> Anyone who claims to be in the light but hates his brother is still in the darkness. Whoever loves his brother lives in the light, and there is nothing in him to make him stumble. But whoever hates his brother is in the darkness and walks around in the darkness; he does not know where he is going, because the darkness has blinded him. *(1 Jn. 2:9–11)*

Similarly, John asserts, 'God is love'. The apostle is not content merely to write that God loves or that his actions are always loving. He uses a more radical expression, which focuses special emphasis: love is so much a part of God's character that the only way to speak of the profundity of his love is to say that he *is* love.

Just as the New Testament encourages us to walk in the light as a result of our knowing God, so it encourages us to walk in love. By definition, John says, 'whoever does not love does not know God' (1 Jn. 4:8).

Once again the point is made. A true understanding of God's nature will have practical consequences. Since both love and light express the heart of God's character, they are also to shape the heart of the Christian life. Truly knowing him will result in a dynamic of renewal – a growing moral purity, a deeper understanding of his will, and a profound love for others.

We have looked at three related ideas: the Old Testament themes of steadfast love and faithfulness, the parallel description of Jesus as 'full of grace and truth', and John's twin themes of love and light.

The biblical message is clear. The God whom Scripture describes, and who reveals himself to us in word and deed, is the God whose nature and actions are perfectly consistent. He does not act on one occasion with love, and on another with justice, or to one generation or individual with compassion, while to another with wrath, as if these qualities were turned on and off according to circumstances or human response. Because truth and love are at the very heart of his nature, he will always act towards us in a way which demonstrates both.

When our attitudes towards others are unforgiving, our responses too selfish, our morality too liberal, or our obedience too casual, we reveal how little we know about God. In his nature, his acts and his words, we come to know and experience the depth of his commitment to us and to our world: perfect love and undiluted truth, working in harmony for our well-being.

Notes

1. Eddie Gibbs, *Winning Them Back* (MARC/Monarch, 1993), p. 74.
2. Quoted in Michael Cole, Jim Graham, Tony Higton and David Lewis, *What is the New Age?* (Hodder and Stoughton, 1990), p. 3.
3. R. T. France, *The Living God* (IVP, 1970), p. 60.
4. D. A. Carson and John D. Woodbridge (eds.), *God and Culture* (Paternoster, 1993), p. 48.
5. Artur Weiser, *The Psalms*, Old Testament Library (SCM, 1962), p. 309.
6. These same terms are used of Christ's ministry. He is described in Hebrews 2:17 as a 'merciful and faithful' high priest. Paul's depiction of Jesus' mission in Romans 15:8–9 also highlights both; Jesus expressed the truth and the mercy of God.

3

Truth in a confused world

It has been estimated that the total media consumption of the average Briton is 75 hours per week. Half of us listen to the radio every day; three-quarters of us read a daily newspaper; and 98% of British households possess at least one television set. Someone has suggested that the British population spends 80 million man hours a week watching soap operas! Not so many of us are like Groucho Marx, who once said that he found television very educating. 'Every time somebody turns on the set, I go into another room and read a book.' For most people, it has the opposite effect. The replacement of the printed page by the television screen, says Neil Postman in his book *Amusing Ourselves to Death*, has eroded our capacity to think clearly about anything. We become absorbed hour after hour, uncritical in our consumption of the relentless flow of images. Television, said Frank Lloyd Wright, is 'chewing gum for the eyes'.

I recently read a comment by a German student who suggested that MTV, the music video satellite channel, was an illusory world. 'It is a flight of the imagination that fulfils a need for fairy tales.'[1] The boundary between fiction and reality blurs. Slumped in a chair with a TV meal or a crate of Guinness, people lose their capacity to evaluate critically the values which are being communicated.

The media are 'the central nervous system of the postmodern body', says Nick Mercer, and they communicate culture. 'The inescapable airwaves shape our thinking from cradle to grave.'[2] It is vital to reflect on how the present cultural climate has shaped our view of what is true, for many Christians find it increasingly difficult to hold firm to God's truth. The distorted impressions portrayed in the media, which are gaining currency at every level of popular culture, make it much harder to hold truth and love together in a way which reflects God's concerns. In this chapter and the next, we shall see that holding to God's truth will mean not only right *thinking* but right *behaviour*, demonstrating that tough minds and tender hearts belong together.

There are three important trends which are now central to our culture and thus reinforced day by day by the subtle but all-pervasive presuppositions of the media: subjectivism, pluralism and relativism. We shall look at these in turn.

'I'm at the centre'

The first trend has been around a long time, and today it is reflected in our exclusive preoccupation with ourselves. Watch the television ads for a while and this obsession becomes blatantly obvious, whether it is to do with the food we eat, the perfume we wear, or the image we must cultivate. Or turn to today's popular books on status, on success as a business executive, and on performance techniques in sex. There is a growing market in books of every kind encouraging self-fulfilment.

The steady development of subjectivism this century has now reached the point where most people conclude that there is no objective meaning at all. While this might sound a little philosophical, in day-to-day life most of us recognize how self-absorbed we are becoming. I can lock myself into my own world with a personal stereo or computer screen. One of my friends spends hours each day surfing the internet. Gradually people are taken over by what becomes a fantasy world, losing touch with reality.

When it comes to matters of right and wrong, truth and falsehood, it is no wonder that in this climate people will naturally declare: 'If it's true for me, it's true.' We create our own reality. We no longer look for the fixed points of religion or social convention to define what is true. I recently read an article on how the Roman Catholic hierarchy was seeking to tackle the wave of scandals that was hitting the church in Ireland. The journalist explained that even the Republic had been influenced by the secular culture to some degree, but that most of all, 'Catholics are becoming more sceptical, more reliant on individual conscience and personal choice'. For the increasing majority, individual choice in matters such as abortion is what matters. Choice becomes a state of mind. No-one really knows the truth, so the ideology of what has come to be known as postmodernity is 'playful indeterminacy'. But too often it becomes a desperate playfulness, laughing for fear we should cry.

This trend in our culture and in the media has led us to believe that 'I am the person who defines reality, who defines right and wrong, true and false'. And this is precisely why New Age is so popular. You pick and mix, you choose what suits you. As the title of a recent article on New Age practice puts it, 'All you need is self-love.'

'Everyone's opinion is valid'

David Cook recounts how, as a Scot arriving in England, he was told that if he wanted to succeed as a professor the secret was to be nice to the students. He duly invited a student and his wife to his home for a meal. The doorbell rang and David welcomed his guests, introducing his wife, whom the student immediately kissed.

In the part of Scotland I come from, when someone else kisses your wife you smash him in the face. However, I did realise that this was not quite the way to begin a deeply meaningful relationship, so I restrained myself. I quickly discovered that this behaviour was not uncommon among the English. After many years I am just about able to behave like everyone else.[3]

There are many variations in patterns of social behaviour across Europe. In some Central European countries, I am greeted with a kiss on each cheek; in some, by three kisses. I am told it has reached five in Paris. In Russia I have sometimes been greeted by pastors with a kiss on the lips. And it extends to many other issues: dress, food and drink, the roles of men and women and the manner of bringing up children.

Most of our cities in Britain display this colourful variety, with their multicultural array of restaurants, places of worship, shops and even cinemas. There can be no doubt that such diversity has greatly enriched the cultural and social life of Britain. But it has also resulted in the notion that what is right and wrong, good and bad, varies. As this way of thinking takes on a life of its own, it develops into an insistence on the part of many that there can be no absolute standard of truth or morality.

We are told that there can be no moral principles that are true for all times and all places, and that it is the height of arrogance for Christians to imply that their view is *the* truth. Christians cannot speak about the Christian faith as a unique revelation, nor can they be rigorous in campaigning for converts.

At this point we do need to distinguish between cultural pluralism and religious pluralism. The first is something I enjoy about living in Oxford: the variety of different cultures and lifestyles. You can choose your restaurant along the Cowley Road – the Bombay Emporium, the Kashmir Halal Tandoori, the Hi-Lo Jamaican Eating House, the Beijing Gourmet, the Mongolian BarBQ, Fat Jack's American Hamburgers, Aziz Indian Cuisine, the Penguin Fish Bar and DJ's Café. Cultural pluralism enriches our lives in all kinds of ways (if only I had the time and money)!

The second, religious pluralism, is a graver matter. It is the belief that

> . . . differences between the religions are not a matter of truth and falsehood, but of different perceptions of the one truth; that to speak of religious beliefs as true or false is inadmissible. Religious belief is a private matter. Each of us is entitled to have – as we say – a faith of our own. This is religious

pluralism and it is a widely held opinion in contemporary British society.[4]

Christian truth, in this view, is to be not rejected but accommodated alongside a range of other 'opinions'. The division between opinion and fact is a common device, with its sharp distinction between the public world of facts and the private world of values and opinions. Since religion belongs to our private world, it is not a matter of truth and falsity; it is to do with one's preferences. Christianity, Buddhism or black magic – it is all a matter of personal taste.

This religious (or philosophical) pluralism is deadly serious. In contrast to the enrichment of cultural pluralism, it is a destructive force. It asserts that any suggestion that a particular religious claim is intrinsically superior to another is necessarily wrong. No matter how contradictory, all are to be welcomed and none excluded. None is to be pronounced true if others are pronounced false.

I have no doubt that we must work much harder at understanding each other's culture, and employ a proper respect for and sensitivity to each person and group in our changing society. In a democracy we are under obligation to allow others to disagree. Christians should support the freedom that encourages such diversity. But we should be aware of the cultural drift which reinforces the further decay of belief in objective truth, with all the moral confusion, intellectual uncertainty and emotional sickness which follow.

'It all depends'

Closely related to these two trends is the third: what is true, good, right or wrong varies from time to time, from place to place, and even from person to person. We call it relativism, and its favourite phrase is, 'It all depends.'

This is an increasingly common attitude to truth, extremely pervasive and appealing. According to this view, truth is 'true' in so far as it is authentic to a particular culture or even sub-culture. For example, the Christian faith is 'true' for Europeans or

Caucasians, in that it has shaped art, literature, cultural values and much else in the western world. But it cannot be held to be true for Indian or Chinese cultures. 'It's fine for you, but don't universalize it, don't absolutize it.'

Allan Bloom's much-acclaimed book on the failure of higher education, *The Closing of the American Mind*, indicates that this disease has thoroughly infiltrated the minds of today's students. His opening sentence observes:

> There is one thing a professor can be absolutely certain of: almost every student entering the university believes, or says he believes, that truth is relative . . . Openness – and the relativism that makes it the only plausible stance in the face of various claims to truth and various ways of life and kinds of human beings – is the great insight of our times. The true believer is the real danger.[5]

In my discussions with non-Christian students today, I rarely encounter the attacks on the Christian faith that were common ten years ago. Not many suggest that science has disproved it, or that the resurrection of Jesus was impossible. Instead, the Christian faith is attacked because of our claim to possess universal, absolute, unchanging truth about God and humankind. It is a claim about reality, the way things are, which is an offence to most people today. D. A. Carson comments that it is no longer possible for 'truth' to have universal acceptance:

> Postmodernity is not especially intolerant of religion, provided that no religion is permitted to talk of universally valid truth. Such talk would be intellectually compromised, culturally disrespectful, fundamentally untenable.[6]

New Age has a similar appeal. There are no ultimate distinctions between right and wrong, truth and error. Truth is one thing for you, and another thing for me. It is finally reduced to phrases like: 'Truth is what I make it'; 'It's true because I like it'; 'It's true because it helps me get along.' Truth becomes a commodity to be moulded to serve my own ends. As G. K.

Chesterton put it: 'When people stop believing in the truth, they don't believe in nothing, they believe in anything.' Mike Gatting, the former England cricket captain, sums it up exactly: 'I believe in a bit of everything – God, the supernatural, ghosts, superstitions, UFOs. I like to keep my options open.'

Such relativism only adds to today's moral confusion. Take the following example from a British university. A student told me she had visited a counselling centre on campus because of a particular emotional difficulty she faced. Part of the advice she received there was to sleep with her boyfriend. As a Christian, she knew this to be wrong, but the counsellor insisted that, if it was functionally helpful, it was legitimate. This kind of 'truth' makes no demands on us, for it is shaped according to the patterns of our desires and convenience. The result is a sense of lostness and confusion that arises from living without guidelines.

Another simple and obvious result is the breakdown of trust. As categories of 'right' and 'wrong' are relativized, we lose our trust in one another. I recently read of the increase in sales in Japan of 'alibi tapes'. Businessmen can purchase a tape recording of assorted background noises – a railway station, an airport departure lounge. Sitting at his office desk, a man can slot the cassette into his pocket memo, telephone his wife and, to suitably convincing background noises, explain to her that he has just missed his train and will be late home. Having effectively deceived her, he can then indulge in any diversion he cares for. The fact that such cassettes are marketed openly does not raise an eyebrow. Who is to say it is 'wrong'?

There are occasional encouraging signs that such moral relativism is unacceptable to many people. At the end of 1995 Britain was shocked by the stabbing to death outside his school gates of headmaster Philip Lawrence, struggling to defend a pupil from a group of thugs. One week before he was murdered he gave an interview:

> I am giving parents what they want: Christian values in their children. We believe there is a difference between right and wrong. There is no relativist position. There is forgiveness, but there is *wrong*. And that is something that parents of

whatever religious background are buying into. It's what their children need.

He made a brave statement and, one week later, a courageous stand. But moral relativism is the dominant creed of the leaders of our society, and as long as it continues to rule, morality will make less and less sense.

The inevitable result of these three trends – 'I'm at the centre', 'Everyone's opinion is valid', 'It all depends' – is that people lose their bearings. They are morally bewildered; they are gullible and uncertain; they are truly 'lost'.

We are in a situation similar to that of the church of the first century. The Roman Empire was a plural society that tolerated a rich variety of private superstitions, but it was hostile towards Christians who declared Jesus' lordship as exclusive. The same is true at this end of the twentieth century.

These popular views of truth have had an inevitable impact on the Christian community. The loss of conviction and of certainty which is a feature of much Christian thinking and writing during this century in part reflects the growing influence of such views. With characteristic wit, Malcolm Muggeridge once pointed out that while it would be rare for a butcher to advocate veget-arianism, 'clergymen with atheistic proclivities are as common as blackberries'.

Today, writers parade their doubts rather than their convic-tions. It has become intellectually more respectable to confess uncertainties than to affirm certainties. The 'readiness to question dogma', observes Lesslie Newbigin, 'is regarded as one of the marks of intellectual maturity and competence'.[7]

The result is that Christians who adhere to the foundation truths of Scripture are frequently mocked as fools. They are regarded as simplistic and dishonest. A typical smear appears in the writing of A. N. Wilson in his 'Counterblast' entitled *Against Religion: Why We Should Try to Live Without It*:

The decent, rational person, trying to make up his mind about some moral or social issue, will recognise that, for the most part, he is floundering about in the dark. He will not hope to be certain of very much, and he will not begin to believe that what he thinks to be right for himself, or right for his society at this particular juncture of history, will be right always and everywhere for all men and women. But this is where the rational man differs from the religious man. The religious believer must believe in the universal applicability of his moral judgements as a rational consequence of his belief in God.[8]

The Christian response must include humility. Christian faith is rooted in revealed and absolute truth, but to affirm this is not to imply that we somehow 'possess' the truth and that there is nothing more to learn. It is not an arrogant assertion of complete enlightenment; there are many areas of agnosticism for thinking Christians, and we should be seeking to learn and understand the dimensions and implications of God's truth throughout our lives. But we do so within the framework of what God has said and done in Christ and his Word, and we should not be afraid to say so. Lesslie Newbigin further comments:

> The relativism which is not willing to speak about truth but only about 'what is true for me' is an evasion of the serious business of living. It is the mark of a tragic loss of nerve in our contemporary culture. It is a preliminary symptom of death.[9]

Some years ago I met a group of Christian students who were bewildered by an unusual experience they had had while witnessing to their Christian faith. They had encountered some devotees of a particular sect on their campus. When they set about explaining how their faith in Christ had resulted in a life-transforming experience of peace, love and joy, they were met with broad smiles. The members of the sect replied that they were very happy to hear the testimony of the Christian students, for they too had peace, love and joy.

After the exchange of experiences, the Christians felt unsure how to proceed. After all, most people are interested in Christian testimony, aware as they are of their own lack of peace, love and joy. In today's world, such stories count for a good deal. But if the sect members shared that 'experience', what was left of their distinctive Christian testimony? The students soon discovered that the most important step in their Christian witness was to return to basics. Christian experience is rooted in truth.

I do not mean to imply that truth is merely a set of propositions, with no relation to experience. Truth in the biblical sense affects the whole person, transforming us as we encounter its living power. In the next chapter we shall emphasize that it is of the essence of evangelical faith that we *experience* the truth in a life-changing way. The Christian faith is nothing if it is not a living experience of God. Luther went so far as to argue that only experience makes a theologian. But the Christian life is not totally subjective. Paul was careful to explain to the Corinthian Christians what he considered to be 'of first importance: that Christ died for our sins . . . that he was buried, [and] that he was raised on the third day according to the Scriptures' (1 Cor. 15:3). These were objective, historical facts. All true Christian experience arises from an encounter with Christ who is the truth, and the objective reality of his person and work is the foundation stone of faith.

Christians are committed to the fact that God has spoken and acted in history, and supremely in Jesus Christ the Truth. To affirm a commitment to truth, and to experience its living reality, is profoundly liberating. It frees us to live as God intended us to live. Most people today ask not 'Is it true?' but 'Does it work?' The wisest evangelistic response in this culture is that the Christian faith works because it shows us how we are meant to live, and liberates and empowers us to do so. We can subsequently explain that this is all the more sure because it is founded on the bedrock of objective truth. Paul's assertion to the Corinthian believers was that the bottom line in any estimate of the Christian faith relates to the objective facts of Christ, his death and resurrection.

In contrast to the three popular trends we have identified, we now turn to three building-blocks in Scripture which go to make up the foundations of reality: God is there, he has spoken, and Jesus is his self-revelation.

God is there

Biblical faith is founded on the fact that there is such a thing as absolute truth which is revealed by God himself. Because there is a living God who speaks and acts, there is objective truth which is applicable to all ages and all places.

Some of the most entertaining passages of the Old Testament are the humorous descriptions of the impotence of human idols over against the dynamic activity of the living God. Today's pluralism is nothing new; Israel was surrounded by foreign deities. There is gentle mockery: 'They have mouths, but cannot speak, eyes, but cannot see' (see Ps. 115:3–8; 135:15–18), and a more ferocious exposé recorded by Isaiah: 'Half of the wood he burns in the fire . . . From the rest he makes a god . . . He prays to it and says, "Save me . . ."' (see Is. 44:9–20; cf. 40:18–2). The contrast is spelt out graphically by Jeremiah:

> Like a scarecrow in a melon patch,
> their idols cannot speak;
> they must be carried
> because they cannot walk.
> Do not fear them;
> they can do no harm
> nor can they do any good . . .
> But the LORD is the true God;
> he is the living God, the eternal King.
> When he is angry, the earth trembles;
> the nations cannot endure his wrath . . .
> But God made the earth by his power;
> he founded the world by his wisdom
> and stretched out the heavens by his understanding.
>
> (Je. 10:5, 10, 12)

By his word the entire universe was created (Ps. 33:6, 9). God's word is described as powerful and effective, not only conveying his will and purpose, but actually accomplishing it (Is. 55:11).

Paul noted that the Thessalonian believers had 'turned to God from idols to serve the living and true God' (1 Thes. 1:9). The heart of the Christian faith is expressed in this immense privilege: the possibility of a living relationship with the infinite yet personal God.

For the Christian, then, the starting-point for a belief in universal and absolute truth is an understanding of the living God, the eternal, rational, loving Creator who brought the universe into being by the word of his power and who communicates with those whom he has made. We are not lost in this world, unable to make sense of the landscape or to read the signposts.

For many people today, there is no possibility of objective facts which can be used for moral decision-making. It is down to feelings and personal choice. Hence the bewilderment and lostness. But those who trust the God who has spoken in his Son and in Scripture are in touch with reality – not a God who is a million miles away, but the living God who shares our life with us, who made us and who loves us, and who will guide us day by day. He has spoken a reliable word that can be trusted completely; as a wise Creator he has given us a framework for decision-making that can be employed in every age. His actions throughout history and across a spectrum of cultures all demonstrate that his love and truth transform individuals, families and even societies.

We can approach our lives, our relationships, our ethical decision-making and our study of politics, science or the arts with the confidence that truth is not merely subjective. As Don Posterski expresses it:

> Christian students welcome the truth about molecules and whatever calculus helps verify. Followers of Jesus have no fear that their faith will fail as they walk into a physics class. They know God wrote the first draft for all physics textbooks when he struck the laws of nature as he created the world. Their confidence rests in knowing that all truth is God's truth, wherever it is found.[10]

God has spoken

The Christian affirms the truth of God's Word written: our second foundation of biblical reality. This commitment to the Bible is not always understood by those outside the Christian faith. Why such apparent devotion to a book?

There is a strong connection between the living God and his Word. The Bible is living and authoritative because the God who spoke that Word is living and authoritative. The Christian submits to the Bible as the absolute truth because it originates with God himself.

Paul speaks of the nature of the Bible in a revealing statement to the Thessalonian believers:

> We . . . thank God continually because, when you received the word of God, which you heard from us, you accepted it not as the word of men, but as it actually is, the word of God, which is at work in you who believe. (1 Thes. 2:13)

This verse tells us three things about the message Paul preached. First, *it originated in God himself.* Paul uses an emphatic phrase, 'gospel *of God*', in verses 8 and 9 of the same chapter. This means that the apostolic message, and by extension the whole Bible, is both authoritative and powerful. If it is the living God who speaks, his Word is not restricted to one age or one culture. Although written to specific people and cultures, its truth is absolute and universal. And Paul underlines the fact that, since it is the Word of God, it is powerful; it is at work in those who believe. Again, Paul's statement about the truth is that it is not cold and distant, but dynamic: the verb means that it 'goes on working'. The Christian view of the truth of Scripture is that it is life-giving, powerful and liberating, freeing us from what is incorrect and enslaving, and leading us into God's good purposes for our lives. Jesus' assertion that 'the truth will set you free' (Jn. 8:32) similarly presses home the point: not only are we set free from living in error, but we discover the true freedom which a relationship with God can give.

Secondly, the Thessalonian Christians *received God's truth as they would a friend*, welcoming it in and making it at home in their lives. We should not keep truth in quarantine, but allow it to transform our minds and shape the way we live. Truth, as we shall see in the next chapter, is something to be *done*. This demands a willingness to sit beneath Scripture, ready to listen with a firm purpose to obey. 'The hallmark of Evangelicals', says John Stott, 'is not so much an impeccable set of words as a submissive spirit, namely their *a priori* resolve to believe and obey whatever Scripture may be shown to teach.'[11]

Devotion to the Bible, then, is not an end in itself. To treat the Bible like that would be similar to swallowing a written prescription rather than taking the medicine. Luther once said that we come to the cradle in order to see the baby. In the same way, our willingness to submit to the authority of Scripture reflects our wish to submit to God himself, to come to know Christ more fully and to experience and enjoy his life.

Thirdly, Paul wrote that *God's word goes on working in those who go on believing*. Truth is powerful because God is present, working through the word he speaks. The Bible itself uses images such as fire, a hammer and a sword to express the dynamic of truth.

In the light of these statements, it is clear that God's truth cannot be diluted in an age of tolerance. In the New Testament there is a right sense of intolerance, even confrontation, when truth is challenged. Paul was perfectly plain and direct: 'Even if we or an angel from heaven should preach a gospel other than the one we preached to you, let him be eternally condemned' (Gal. 1:8). The reason for his passion was the burning conviction that the truth was the transforming power of God. It had gripped him, shaped his life, and was turning the world upside down. Now, as then, says Os Guinness, it is this 'which lifts Christianity out of the common pool of completely personal, relativistic, subjective beliefs'.[12]

The image of God

We turn now to our third foundation of Christian reality. Truth is expressed supremely, not in a system or in a series of propositions, but in a person, Jesus Christ. In the last chapter we saw how John declared that Jesus not only claimed to teach and bear witness to the truth, but was himself the truth. He is full of grace and truth. He is the way, the truth and the life (Jn. 14:6). Let us explore John's presentation of Jesus as the truth.

First, *Jesus is the truth about God*. Just like us, John lived in a confused world offering many answers to the question: 'How can we find out about God?' The Greeks argued for a rational approach to seeking ultimate truth. The mystery religions saw religious experience as the means by which to tap the spiritual energies behind the universe. The people of John's day knew all about religious pluralism, and he challenged his culture by clearly presenting Jesus Christ. We come to know God not solely through reason, or through mystical experience, but through a Person.

God has spoken his 'Word', as John explains in the first chapter of his gospel. 'No one has ever seen God; the only Son . . . has made him known' (Jn. 1:18, RSV). Jesus was the eternal Word who became the incarnate Word: 'The Word became flesh and made his dwelling among us. We have seen his glory, the glory of the One and Only, who came from the Father, full of grace and truth' (1:14).

Jesus' claim to be the truth means that he says to us: 'If you want to know the truth about God, look at me. If you want to hear God's Word, listen to me.' Other religions believe in an eternal word, but at its highest this is only verbal communication. The Muslim, for example, pays great respect to the text of Allah's dictation to Muhammad. But the fullest expression of the eternal Word of God is not a divine book but a divine Person.

Secondly, *Jesus reveals the truth about the Father*. 'I am the way and the truth and the life. No-one comes to the Father except through me' (Jn. 14:6). We come to know the truth about God as Father not through a principle, or by a force, but through Jesus Christ. He not only reveals the truth of what it means to be made right with God; he is himself the way into God's presence. This is best understood by returning once again to the expression 'grace and truth', used in John 1:14, 17. Jesus reveals to us the truth about ourselves, the truth about the Father, and the truth of salvation. And he reveals God's grace in opening the way into

God's presence, in forgiving us and in cleansing us through his own person and work.

Thirdly, *Jesus is the centre-point of all truth.* Paul described the purpose of his energetic work: 'that they may be encouraged in heart and united in love, so that they may have the full riches of complete understanding, in order that they may know the mystery of God, namely, Christ, in whom are hidden all the treasures of wisdom and knowledge' (Col. 2:2–3).

Some while ago the makers of a breakfast cereal offered a free gift. Our family had to eat several packets of the stuff because the children were so intrigued. The company was giving away '3D specs' – special glasses which, once balanced on your nose, transformed a confused picture on the cereal box into a three-dimensional work of art in living colour. Paul's point in Colossians 2 is that the truth about Christ is the one thing that makes sense of everything else in creation. He is the Creator and Lord of all, and therefore his self-revelation brings truth into focus. Whatever we understand about the natural world is ultimately to do with his creative wisdom and power. John says the same in his prologue: 'Through him all things were made; without him nothing was made that has been made' (Jn. 1:3).

For the Christian, knowing Christ provides the lens through which we see life as a whole: not just the religious or 'spiritual' part, but all things. The centrality of Christ provides us with the perspective from which we can begin to determine our response to moral and social issues, relationships, marriage, work, church life, past, present and future. The way to know truth, then, is to enter a living relationship with Christ himself. As Oliver Barclay points out:

> One amazing result of this, for which we must all be deeply thankful, is that you do not have to be clever to have a profound faith. Even a simple child can have the heart of the matter and can have grasped the unifying theme of all theology, ethics and philosophy, because he can have a personal faith in Jesus Christ as the one who is above all and 'in whom are hidden all the treasures of wisdom and knowledge'.[13]

This is very different from commitment to ideology alone.

There is nothing abstract about biblical truth. We have pressed the point several times: truth is alive and has power to set people free. It is in knowing Jesus Christ the Truth that we come to understand the wisdom and knowledge which God has revealed and which liberate those who willingly bow their knee to him.

Our response

In drawing the chapter to a close, we might reflect upon three simple responses to the Christian view of truth which we have been considering. We must be certain of the gospel; sensitive in communicating it; and prayerful as we seek to persuade others of its truth.

Certainty

We have seen that for Paul the central truths of the gospel were 'of first importance'. Our response must be to understand the gospel clearly and to commit ourselves to Christ and his lordship. This means being committed to biblical faith: to Christ as the unique incarnation of God and only Saviour, and to his Word as authoritative for all ages and all times.

The early Christians faced the challenge of many conflicting claims to truth. Theirs was one faith, young and apparently weak, among many. But they adopted a position of 'no compromise'. This did not involve imposing their views or acting in an arrogant manner, but it did mean standing with certainty for the exclusive claims of their faith because they loved Christ and were empowered by his Spirit.

Sensitivity

To believe in the uniqueness of the Christian revelation does not entail adopting a 'crusading spirit'. We are not imperialists, dismissing other people's cultures. We should not be aggressive in our evangelistic style. We do not judge every claim of every other religion to be false or completely empty and without value. Christian conviction about the truth should lead to humility and compassion. It will leave room for listening and for dialogue, and an openness to others that is characterized by gentleness – even towards those with whom we might strongly disagree. These are themes which we shall explore in later chapters, but we need to underline here that an understanding of Christian truth, and a commitment to Christ who is the focal point of that truth, will demonstrate themselves most clearly in lives which are modelled on Jesus himself.

Prayer and persuasion

'Since, then, we know what it is to fear the Lord, we try to persuade men' (2 Cor. 5:11). The apostles were so gripped by the power of truth and of love that they preached, persuaded, and pleaded with people to turn to Christ. So must we. We are Christ's ambassadors, not neutral observers. We appeal to people to be reconciled to God. While this might mean offering a critique of the relativism and pluralism of our day, it will certainly involve a commitment to prayer. Alongside his encouragement to the Corinthian believers to act as Christ's ambassadors and to 'set forth the truth plainly', Paul reminded them that 'the god of this age has blinded the minds' of men and women 'so that they cannot see the light of the gospel of the glory of Christ' (2 Cor. 4:1–6). Through prayer we can ask the Lord to use our witness to Christ and, by the power of his Word and his Spirit, transform the lives of our friends who have not yet discovered 'the truth that is in Jesus' (Eph. 4:21).

We live in a broken and confused world. There will be a few people around us who hold vigorously to a philosophical position such as relativism or pluralism, but most are simply bewildered. They may have drawn the conclusion that in this supermarket of ideas there is nothing worth having, little comfort or help for their lives and very little security in a world where everything is changing. For such friends and neighbours, what is needed most of all is pastoral evangelism – a compassion such as Jesus had for those who were like sheep without a shepherd (Mk. 6:34); a steady faithfulness in building genuine friendships; and a demonstration by our lives and our words that we have found him who is the truth.

I have already implied that for many people 'truth' has become irrelevant. They need to see how the gospel meets their needs, and how its message is relevant and attractive. The most convincing evidence for Christian truth in our day is not only a clear and relevant presentation of the facts of the gospel, but Christians who live under the authority of that truth, giving credible evidence of the reality of Christ and his love. The truth of God is good news in an age of uncertainty and, in Christ, the transforming personal power for a world in desperate need of liberation and guidance. In the next chapter we shall examine how we should demonstrate that reality – for truth is alive and well. It is not a rule-book but an explosive; not a set of propositions but a Person.

Notes

1. Quoted in Gavin McGrath, *Confident Christianity* (IVP, 1995), p. 64.
2. Nick Mercer, *Mission and Meaning* (Paternoster, 1995), p. 331.
3. David Cook, *Dilemmas of Life* (IVP, 1990), p. 57.
4. Lesslie Newbigin, *The Gospel in a Pluralist Society* (SPCK, 1989), p. 14.
5. Allan Bloom, *The Closing of the American Mind* (Penguin, 1988), pp. 25–26.
6. D. A. Carson, *The Gagging of God* (Apollos, 1996), pp. 347–348.
7. Newbigin, *The Gospel in a Pluralist Society*, p. 5.
8. A. N. Wilson, *Against Religion*, Chatto Counterblasts 19 (Chatto and Windus, 1991), p. 10.
9. Newbigin, *The Gospel in a Pluralist Society*, p. 22.
10. Don Posterski, *Studying Jesus' Way* (IVCF Canada), p. 11.
11. David L. Edwards and John Stott, *Essentials* (Hodder and Stoughton, 1988), p. 104.
12. Os Guinness, *God in the Dark* (Hodder and Stoughton, 1996), p. 67.
13. O. R. Barclay, *Developing a Christian Mind* (IVP, 1984), p. 55, quoting Col. 2:3.

Truth in action

Taxi-drivers are often the first people one meets in a new country, and they can usually be relied upon to offer a crisp observation about the culture. I sat in the back of one smoke-filled cab and we drove off from the airport. I knew a few Russian words and asked the driver about one of the best-known: *perestroika*. Air exploded from his lips and both hands left the wheel. Today Russians look back on the heyday of that word with more than a degree of cynicism.

In his book *Perestroika*, Mikhail Gorbachev made frequent reference to the credibility gap between words and deeds. He insisted that people did not want political slogans that failed to square with reality. *Perestroika* meant 'the unity of words and deeds', and on this basis Gorbachev attempted to reform the Soviet system. It was a noble aim. For most of the citizens of the USSR, however, its failure was all too evident. Gorbachev had been unable to deliver. The hoped-for unity between political promises and economic and social reality was a myth. And, as in the case of many before him and doubtless many more to follow, therein lay Gorbachev's downfall.

Manifesto pledges and political programmes are empty unless we see genuine change in the real world where most of us live. The same principle is heralded in the new styles of management in the business world. Charles Handy in *The Age of Unreason* highlights a key principle of leadership: 'The leader must *live* the vision.' Leaders must be people of integrity, demonstrating their belief by the way they live.

This is exactly the test that the Bible introduces. 'By their fruit you will recognise them' (Mt. 7:16, 20). In a remarkably demanding challenge, the apostle John states: 'Whoever claims to live in him must walk as Jesus did' (1 Jn. 2:6).

When I was ten years old I was involved in a small church in north London where my father was one of the elders. I owe much to that faithful group of believers. But it was the place where, with a degree of shock I can still recall, I first encountered failure in the Christian community. It was discovered that the church treasurer had embezzled funds over a period of years. In a small fellowship where everyone knew each other, its impact was considerable. Being a child, I was not party to all that went on. But the emotional impact is something I remember well: a prominent Christian leader in our congregation had deceived people; someone we had seen as beyond failure had acted so inconsistently.

Looking back on the experience, I must add that the situation was dealt with in a very gracious and firm manner. The brother in question was eventually restored, and with extraordinary humility he served the church in many ways in the years that followed. I respected him and the church leaders enormously. But this crisis brought my first exposure to this key principle: those who name the name of Christ must *live* his life.

Living a lie

In the Old Testament, one of the things that deeply disturbed the prophet Jeremiah was the appalling failure of the so-called prophets of his day. These were men who should have spoken the word of God fearlessly at a time of spiritual decline and moral confusion. They were called by the Lord not only to speak the truth but to live it.

What sent Jeremiah reeling was that, instead of providing leadership in a time of crisis and directing people away from sin, they actually confirmed them in it.

> The prophets follow an evil course . . .
> Both prophet and priest are godless;
>> even in my temple I find their wickedness,
>>> declares the LORD.
> Among the prophets of Jerusalem
>> I have seen something horrible:
>>> they commit adultery and live a lie.
> They strengthen the hands of evildoers,
>> so that no one turns from his wickedness.
>
> *(Je. 23:10–11, 14)*

It was clear to Jeremiah, if not to God's people, that the behaviour of the false prophets was the exact opposite of what was required of God's spokesmen. As John Goldingay remarks: 'A true prophet will be one whose own life is an embodiment of the truth.'[1]

Consistent living

James is one of the New Testament writers who is concerned about godliness in working clothes. He would be much more at home on a bus than in a stained-glass window, and much more concerned about real Christians than about religious fakes. In the first chapter of his letter he explains the importance of action as evidence of true faith. He does so with a series of examples, the first two of which describe religious fakes.

The *armchair Christian* (Jas. 2:14–17) is full of good advice, but will not lift a finger to help. He has all the spiritual jargon and all the right Bible texts, but no action. 'What good is it, my brothers, if a man claims to have faith but has no deeds?'

The *demons* are also false believers, says James (2:19). Something of a shock to his religious readers, this one! How could they possibly be compared to demons? In this way: demons have an orthodox doctrinal position, but they do not have genuine faith, which means believing in Christ with trust *and* obedience. The demons believe, but they carry on in their wickedness. Be careful not to do the same, James insists.

Then he puts forward two examples of genuine faith. Both are from Old Testament history. One was a Jew and the other a Gentile; one a man of great godliness and the other a woman and a prostitute. But both of them had saving faith, faith that works.

The first was *Abraham* (2:21–24). His act of obedience in offering his son Isaac demonstrated that his faith in God was the real thing. The genuineness of our faith is proved in actions, and provides the basis for our being declared righteous before God. 'It is faith alone that justifies,' said Calvin, 'but faith that justifies is never alone.'

James's second positive example is *Rahab* (2:25). She believed that God was the only true God, and she proved that her faith was genuine by caring for the spies sent to Jericho. Hebrews 11 lists the great heroes of faith – spiritual giants, true people of God, upstanding and respectable. Listed there is Rahab the hooker. Despite the risks, she demonstrated her faith by actions.

James sums up his point with a good question: 'Who is wise and understanding among you?' (3:13). We might imagine that wisdom and understanding imply a sure intellectual grasp of the truth. And well they might. But how does James answer his question? 'Let him show it by his good life, by deeds done in the humility that comes from wisdom.'

Living in conformity with God's character

In chapter 2 we examined the qualities of God's character expressed in three phrases: his steadfast love and faithfulness; Jesus, full of grace and truth; and John's use of the metaphors of love and light. If we have come to know God, and to express genuine faith in him, then we are called to reflect those same qualities and to live in conformity with God's character. The truth is dynamic and life-changing, and so, as 'mirrors of God', we are called to *do* truth, not simply to believe it.

Being 'sound' doctrinally is usually to invite gentle mockery these days. The word has had something of a bad press. It implies dull orthodoxy, a lack of imagination, conservatism at its worst. But this misses the point entirely. 'Sound' teaching is healthy teaching. It is truth which produces wholeness and godliness. In his letter to Titus, Paul encourages sound doctrine by illustrating its impact in moral, sexual, domestic and social life (2:1ff.). It is fundamental to our integrity as Christians, 'so that those who oppose you may be ashamed because they have nothing bad to say about us' (2:7–8).

The opening verse of his letter makes the connection: 'Paul, a servant of God and an apostle of Jesus Christ for the faith of God's elect and the knowledge of *the truth that leads to godliness*' (1:1). As Anthony Thiselton observes: 'Purity of life constitutes part of the grammar of truth.'[2]

Just as truth demands such a life, so does love. The centrality of love in God's character is matched by its centrality in the Christian life: we are to be 'rooted and grounded in love' (Eph. 3:17, RSV). It should be the root of all of our actions and the foundation on which the church is built. The test of truth is this: does it produce godliness? The test of love is the same: 'Dear children, let us not love with words or tongue but with actions and in truth' (1 Jn. 3:18).

John's three letters are full of encouragements to exactly this kind of consistent Christian living. With directness and simplicity, the commands John presents to us are invitations to understand and to live in the light of God's character. Since he is the God whose nature is steadfast love and faithfulness, and since he has demonstrated the reality and dynamic power of these attributes in his saving mercy, so God's people must live out these qualities in radical action.

If God is light, then the Christian life means walking in the light (1 Jn. 1:6–7). If God is truth, the Christian life is walking in the truth (2 Jn. 4; 3 Jn. 3). And if he is love, then it is walking in love (also described as walking in obedience, 2 Jn. 6).

Belief and practice

To walk in the light means that the whole of my life is shaped by God's standards – the way I think, but also the way I act. It is impossible for light and darkness to co-exist in the same place, as the apostle states. Since God is light, it is impossible to know him, love him and serve him, if at the same time I am living in darkness (1 Jn. 1:6). Here John introduces the phrase which is the theme of this chapter: 'live by the truth'. Elsewhere he uses other expressions to convey the same idea: 'does the will of God' (2:17), 'do what pleases him' (3:22), 'does what is right' (2:29; 3:7). It means more than 'practising what you preach'. Truth includes both orthodoxy (right belief) and orthopraxy (right practice). It means living wholeheartedly in conformity with the character of God. If we are united with the Godhead, then our whole lives – our character and our behaviour – will be shaped by God's active truth and empowered by his love.

It is important to stress that this is a dynamic, life-changing commitment to truth, not merely an academic conviction. The truth is actively at work within us, as we emphasized in the last chapter (*cf.* 1 Thes. 2:13), transforming us more and more into conformity with God's character. C. S. Lewis captured the force of walking in the light when he wrote: 'We might think that God wanted simply obedience to a set of rules; whereas he really wants people of a particular sort.'

Word and deed

We all know how important this transformation of life is in today's world. If we Christians are known for anything, it tends to be for preaching the gospel rather than for living it. Martin Luther King once described the persistent schizophrenia of Christians who proudly profess certain sublime principles but practise the very antithesis of those principles: 'How often our lives are characterised by a high blood pressure of creeds and an anaemia of deeds!'[3] But we live in an age increasingly weary of talk that is not accompanied by action. Maybe you have seen the graffito above the hot-air hand-dryer in a public WC: 'Press the button for a message from the Prime Minister.'

Truth has to be spoken, of course. Paul frequently uses the term 'truth' as shorthand for the gospel of Christ – something to be proclaimed (Rom. 9:1; 2 Cor. 12:6). John opens his first letter with the words: 'We proclaim to you what we have seen and heard, so that you also may have fellowship with us' (1 Jn. 1:3–4). The experience of eternal life is impossible without hearing the preaching of the apostolic word, the verbal witness to the truth.

John is determined to correct false teaching, not least because it leads to false living. Truth is indeed something to be told. But both James and John tell us that faith in the gospel means obedient faith, truth in action.

John develops this further in his second and third letters. In both, he expresses the theme with the phrase 'walking in the truth', which means not only believing in the truth of Christ, but actively seeking to bring the whole of our lives into subjection to it.

A brief look at 3 John will help us understand what this means. He gives us a glimpse of first-century church life – the good, the bad and the ugly. We shall easily recognize it, for many of our churches and personal relationships are characterized by remarkably similar features. He frequently stresses that conviction and compassion belong together. The opening verses of the letter introduce five ideas which have immediate reference to our theme.

Christians are held together by truth and love

First, John addresses his dear friend Gaius as one 'whom I *love in the truth*' (3 Jn. 1). He uses the same phrase in 2 John 1, and here again demonstrates how true Christian fellowship expresses the partnership of love and truth. It was the truth that is in Jesus that tied John and Gaius together in love. The idea has added force when we notice the particularly affectionate way in which John addresses his 'friend' (verses 2, 5, 11, and also 1 Jn. 2:7; 3:21; 4:3, 7): he uses the word 'beloved' (as some translations have it, since the Greek word is derived from *agapē*, the distinctive Christian word for 'love').

It is worth pausing here to reflect on our own experience of Christian fellowship. Our congregations are frequently made up of an extraordinary mix of people who, at the human level, seem to stand relatively little chance of working together effectively. In the churches to which I have belonged, I have come to realize what a wonderful thing it is that the gospel unites me with people who, in normal circumstances, I would never have dreamt of meeting, let alone befriending. I am sure they think the same about me. Were the church a purely human organization, we would undoubtedly be heading for trouble.

Sadly, of course, churches are often the arena for friction and interpersonal conflict. But John's simple phrase is a timely reminder for all of us who are tempted to lose sight of the fact that the Christian community has been brought together, not as a club for the like-minded, but as the fellowship of Christ created by the Holy Spirit, a new society supernaturally given birth by the gospel of truth and love. As John White describes it:

> The genius of Christianity is that it makes possible ongoing fellowship between people who could not otherwise tolerate, let alone enjoy one another. Christ gets refined socialites hobnobbing with migrant farm workers; middle-aged squares weeping with rebels and swingers; blacks, Indians, Jews and wasps praying earnestly together, and management and labour sharing each other's problems. In a world divided by class, commerce, race, education, politics, the generation gap and a million clashing interests, Christ alone can make incompatibles mesh.[4]

Christians should live out the truth

Secondly, John refers to Gaius as one who walks in the truth (3 Jn. 3–4). We have already seen how John uses the phrase to describe consistent Christian living. Now, both here and in 2 John 4, he expresses thanksgiving for those who are determined to live out the truth. Gaius was that kind of person. He demonstrated the truth of what he believed by his lifestyle.

This is what the world is looking for and yet so often misses in Christianity. It is why our prime apologetic today is the attractiveness of the gospel seen in Christian lives and Christian community. Walking in the truth is the essential requirement of all who name the name of Christ. He was 'mighty in word and deed'. There was about him no hint of inconsistency or religious hypocrisy. He lived the truth, and he calls us to do the same. And if, after having come to the light, we 'do the truth', we shall have no fear when others examine our lives or witness our behaviour. To live by the truth is to allow the Lord Jesus to do the truth through us, 'so that it may be seen plainly that what he has done has been done through God' (Jn. 3:21). It is one of the most important tests of the genuineness of our faith. As we face a watching world, living the truth is all-important.

There is a humorous incident in the story of Karen Blixen, a Danish Christian whose book *Out of Africa* was filmed with Meryl Streep in the leading role. Blixen records that it was an alarming experience to be – in her own person – representing Christianity to the natives.

> There was a young Kikuyu by the name of Kitau, who came in from the Kikuyu Reserve and took service with me. He was a meditative boy, an observant, attentive servant, and I liked him well. After three months he one day asked me to give him a letter of recommendation to my old friend Sheik Ali bin Salim, the *Lewali* of the Coast, at Mombasa, for he had seen him in my house and now, he said, he wished to go and work for him. I did not want Kitau to leave just when he had learned the routine of the house, and I said to him that I would rather raise his pay. No, he said, he was not leaving to get any higher pay, but he could not stay. He told me he had made up his mind, up in the Reserve, that he would become either a Christian or a Mohammedan, only he did not yet know which. For this reason he had come and worked for me, since I was a Christian, and he had stayed for three months in my house to see the *testurde* – the ways and habits – of the Christians. From me he would go for three months to Sheik Ali in Mombasa and study the *testurde* of the Mohammedans; then he would decide. I believe even an archbishop, when he had had these facts laid before him, would have said, or at least have thought, as I said: 'Good God, Kitau, you might have told me that when you came here.'[5]

Christians should demonstrate costly love

Thirdly, Gaius expressed his commitment to the truth through demonstrating practical love towards other believers (3 Jn. 5–6). He was known as someone to whom the truth mattered. His walking in truth meant walking in love. Gaius's love matched the truth. It was evident in his generous hospitality to 'strangers', the term John uses for itinerant preachers and missionaries.

Hospitality may at first seem a relatively simple and rather unglamorous point for John to highlight. But all those who have opened their home over a long period of time, or given sacrificially for God's work, know the personal costs and inconveniences that this can involve. It is one of the tests of sincere love. A friend of mine defines the gift of hospitality as 'making people feel at home when you wish they were'!

Faithfulness in these modest but demanding tasks is part of our Christian calling. We are reflecting in some small way the generous and sacrificial love of God towards us. When such commitment is demonstrated in today's world, it can have a powerful impact for the cause of the gospel. Our generosity to those in need is simply an act of obedience to the command and example of the Lord Jesus, as John reminds us:

> This is how we know what love is: Jesus Christ laid down his life for us. And we ought to lay down our lives for our brothers. If anyone has material possessions and sees his brother in need but has no pity on him, how can the love of God be in him? Dear children, let us not love with words or tongue but with actions and in truth.   *(1 Jn. 3:16–18)*

Samuel Logan Brengle, a Methodist minister in the States, received a call from William Booth to cross the Atlantic and join him in the early days of the Salvation Army. Brengle decided to leave his large congregation, and reported for duty in London. Booth immediately gave him the job of cleaning the boots of the other recruits. Brengle records the sense of humiliation he felt. Had he left a prestigious ministry and crossed the Atlantic just to clean boots? And then he described how, almost as if in a vision, he saw Jesus, bending over the feet of rough fishermen. 'Lord,' he said, 'you washed their feet; I will black their boots.'

Jesus laid down his life for us. We ought to lay down our lives for others.

Fourthly, John describes Gaius's faithfulness towards visiting missionaries. The expression he uses indicates that, by such practical help, we 'play our part in spreading the truth' (3 Jn. 8, NEB). Moffatt translates the phrase, 'allies to the Truth'. Once again John is pressing home his point: commitment to the truth will mean action.

It is relatively easy, as James has shown us, to say that we believe in the gospel. We might repeat the Apostles' Creed Sunday by Sunday; we might affirm our agreement with a doctrinal statement by our signature; we might be familiar with evangelical jargon and convince others of our orthodoxy. But John will not let us get away with merely this. The essence of commitment to the truth will mean not only belief and verbal affirmation, but also practical action, transformed lifestyles and compassionate service. In 3 John he mentions specific practical care for missionaries, but his letters show us that he has a wide concern for loving action of all kinds.

Some of the most powerful evangelism in the member movements of the International Fellowship of Evangelical Students[6] has arisen from a radical and practical commitment to the truth. It is Christian witness with integrity. In Peru, Christian students and graduates have formed a National Evangelical Commission to care for the needy. They look after the orphans of pastors and Christian workers who have been killed by the guerrillas; Christian graduates in psychology have used their skills to establish a counselling service to help the bereaved overcome their trauma; Christian law graduates have set up a legal commission to provide defence for poor Christians who are falsely accused and wrongly imprisoned. They have combined direct evangelistic ministry with high ethical standards, a developed social conscience and practical action.

In Uganda, Christian graduates have established an Aids programme of education, counselling and day workshops. Their care and behavioural-change programme has been used in churches and colleges. They have also committed themselves to the care of over 200 disadvantaged children in their Children's

Centre Project. In Kenya, Christian students have entered the UN camps for refugees, giving literacy classes and training refugees in activities that will generate income. Even modest projects can be established to demonstrate the truth in action: in Chile, students set up a cafeteria service for others who could not afford good meals. All these Christians are *allies for the truth*, making the gospel attractive.

This leads us to one final phrase in John's short letter which also has a bearing on our theme.

Christians should be totally consistent

When Paul wrote to the Thessalonian believers, he had to defend himself against the charges of those false teachers who implied that he was involved in Christian ministry only for personal gain and prestige. Several times he referred to the fact that his life had been blameless, and he was bold enough to suggest that not only they, the Thessalonian Christians, were witnesses of this fact, but so too was God (1 Thes. 2:5, 10). Much the same could be said of Demetrius, mentioned in 3 John 12. He was 'well spoken of by everyone'. But more than that: in addition to the witness of those who knew him well, the truth itself joined in that testimony. What did John mean?

It was a remarkable commendation. Demetrius lived in conformity with God's truth to such an extent that he did not really need the testimony of fellow Christians to vouch for his consistent lifestyle. It was self-evident; the truth itself confirmed that here was a man who 'did the truth'. No other witnesses were needed.

This is what Paul refers to as making the truth attractive (Tit. 2:10). In an age when so many are sceptical about the Christian faith, we need to take seriously the biblical encouragements to proclaim the truth with clarity as we testify to the Lord Jesus, and to support and enhance such witness with lives that embody the truth. 'Whatever happens, conduct yourselves in a manner worthy of the gospel of Christ' (Phil. 1:27).

This, then, is how we should 'walk' as Christians. As the

American evangelist D. L. Moody put it: 'Every Bible should be bound in shoe leather.'

Notes

1. John Goldingay, *God's Prophet, God's Servant* (Paternoster, 1984), p. 50.
2. Anthony Thiselton, *Interpreting God and the Postmodern Self* (T. and T. Clark, 1996), p. 37.
3. Martin Luther King, *Strength to Live* (Fontana, 1969), p. 37.
4. John White, *The Fight* (IVP, 1977), p. 135.
5. Karen Blixen, *Out of Africa* (Penguin, 1985), p. 47.
6. The International Fellowship of Evangelical Students (IFES) is a partnership of some 130 national student movements, seeking to encourage Christian students to witness to their fellow students in universities worldwide.

Love in a broken world

The film *Sleepless in Seattle* was a huge box-office success in the States and around the world. This romantic comedy said a great deal about the state of relationships in our culture, and the plot was especially appropriate. Set in the 'love-starved 90s', it was about the love of a young woman for a man she had never met, hearing his voice on a lonely-hearts phone-in radio show. They lived on opposite sides of the country, one in Seattle and one in Baltimore.

At about the same time as the film was released, Allan Bloom, the American academic, published a book about love and friendship. In it, he observed: 'Isolation, a lack of profound contact with other human beings, seems to be the disease of our time. We are lonely while living in society, with all the social needs of others, yet unable to satisfy them.'

It is not only in the USA where relationships are increasingly dysfunctional. We in Europe are living in societies where love, friendship and genuine community are withering. The tone is captured by Erich Fromm in his book *The Sane Society*: 'There is not so much love to be found in the world of our day. There is rather a superficial friendliness, concealing a distance, an indifference, a subtle distrust.'

A friend of ours lived in a block of flats not far from our home.

Although she was surrounded by people, she once told us that she felt she 'knew' the characters in *Coronation Street* better than she knew her neighbours along the corridor. She longed for human friendship, yet felt emotionally isolated. As Mother Teresa once described western society, 'There is no hunger for bread, but there are people suffering from terrible loneliness, terrible despair, terrible hatred, feeling unwanted, feeling helpless, feeling hopeless.' We are hungry for love.

But how are we to understand the word? In the West we have inherited the view that love is nearly always to do with sexual passion. We speak about love between the sexes, an overpowering emotion that has little to do with the will. We 'fall in love'. The word has strong romantic overtones, with full orchestral backing. But this is far removed from the Christian concept of love.

If our lives are to reflect God's character, combining his love and truth, it is essential that we restore a proper understanding of what Christian love is all about. We have seen that holding to God's truth in our thinking and our action is powerful and attractive – and so it should be, reflecting as it does the character of God and the image of Christ. But what of love? Has our culture once again distorted our Christian understanding and commitment?

Let us turn again to the apostle John. In his first letter alone, he uses the verb and the noun for 'love' nearly fifty times. How does he define the word? 'This is how we know what love is: Jesus Christ laid down his life for us' (1 Jn. 3:16). 'This is love: not that we loved God, but that he loved us and sent his Son as an atoning sacrifice for our sins' (4:10).

This is a love shaped by duty. It has nothing to do with the sentimental, the erotic or the romantic. When John refers to God's love, he is talking about Jesus on the cross. It is determined love. It expresses a commitment to action and to sacrifice. He is making clear that love is not simply what we feel but what we do.

Much more can be said about the dimensions of love, of course. It would be quite wrong to suggest that we should have no feelings. In that great hymn to love in 1 Corinthians 13, Paul says that love *rejoices* in the truth. Our love for the Lord is something that should provoke 'inexpressible joy' (1 Pet. 1:8), so love clearly involves our affections as well as our decisions. (We shall pick up the theme of passion in the final chapter.)

The Greek language has the benefit of various words to describe the full range of meaning of our word 'love'. They provide a precision that our one English word lacks.

The word *storgē* describes natural or family love. This kind of affection is an important dimension of love, but was not the word chosen by the New Testament writers. Christian love is more than just a family tie.

Then there is *philia*, which means the love of friendship. It is used only once in the New Testament (for friendship with the world, in Jas. 4:4) and, while it is an essential ingredient in our lives, again it is not the term employed to describe Christian love. The verb *phileō* is used frequently, but generally to refer to human love associated with friendship. As such it represents a noble quality, but it does not express the idea of God's love for the unworthy, and so it does not capture the essential New Testament idea of love.

Epithymia refers to strong desire, even passionate love. It is used for both positive and negative ideas in the Bible (for Jesus' desire to eat the Passover with his disciples, but also for lust and coveting), but is not usually translated by the word 'love'.

Erōs is not found in the New Testament at all, although it is the best-known Greek word for 'love'. There are two basic characteristics of *erōs*: it is the love which sees something worthy (beauty in the eye of the beholder) and that longs for possession. Again, such love can be profound and a valuable part of our lives. Romantic love is described in the Song of Songs in positive terms. There is nothing essentially evil about it, since love between the sexes is a wonderfully positive aspect of God's good creation. But once again it is not the word chosen to describe the distinctive Christian idea of love.

The New Testament writers had to describe a new category of love, and they chose the word *agapē*. Here was a general word for 'love', unemotional and uncluttered, which they could define in uniquely Christian terms. It was not a love of the worthy, or a love that desires to possess, but a love that seeks to give, a love that is committed even to sacrifice.

Since we have been so influenced by other views of love, we often react against the concept of love as sacrifice. It seems too extreme. On one occasion I led a discussion group with non-Christians in a small Devon village near my home. The subject I had been given was 'Marriage and the family'. We looked at Paul's description of marriage relationships in Ephesians 5, in which he draws a parallel between the husband's love for a wife, and Christ's commitment to the church. Paul was being deliberately radical in drawing the comparison, for Christ 'gave himself' for the church. Love, I suggested to the group, is sacrificial. At that point one of the women present exploded with anger. For her, the language of sacrifice was shocking; it was entirely inappropriate for human relationships in today's world. Such a view, she insisted, would lead to abuse of all kinds, and to being taken advantage of. It would make us dangerously vulnerable.

I could not judge what led her to react in this way. Many of us are deeply wounded by our marriages and family relationships, and we use various self-defence mechanisms to protect ourselves from being wounded still further. But I had gently to underline that the New Testament view of love has sacrifice at its heart. John's description of God's love implies that it will be the victim rather than the predator; it will be the giver rather than the beneficiary; it will take the initiative rather than wait for others; it will be concerned with duty and responsibility rather than rights. The reaction of my non-Christian friend was understandable in a world which is shaped by the demanding, hungry love which always looks out for itself rather than for others. I do not stand apart from her view as if innocent or uncontaminated. I am caught up in the same self-centred little world; I have the same desire to protect myself from harm, and to secure maximum self-gratification at every turn.

But why did Jesus come? John's description of God's love removes the saccharin and sentimentality, the self-centredness and the merely emotional. Jesus made it clear in Luke 6 that love is not simply a matter of loving those who love us. Even sinners do that! Real love has not begun until it is sacrificial – responding with grace when people hate us, replying positively when people slander us, praying for someone who curses us. This kind of love is what Jesus demonstrated, going beyond the ordinary to the extraordinary.

As we have stressed in the opening chapters of this book, our understanding of love depends upon our understanding of God. 'We will discover what love is all about', writes Michael Harper, 'only when we allow ourselves to be divested of all assumed concepts which may have come from non-Christian sources, and seek to know God and find in him and his action the real meaning.'[1]

In this chapter we shall examine three themes: the nature of love as seen in God's character and actions; the priority of genuine love within the Christian life; and finally the obligations of love, which will bring us full circle to the theme of compassion and conviction.

God's love

One of the great songs celebrating the rich dimensions of God's steadfast love is Psalm 136, with its unique refrain, 'His love endures for ever', running throughout. There are several features worth noting.

Persistent love

The word for 'love' in the refrain is the word we have met already in chapter 2 – God's steadfast love (*ḥeseḏ*). It describes his special care for those to whom he is bound in covenant relationship. His love for us is entirely dependable.

We rarely use the psalm as we should, with a leader singing the first line of each verse and the congregational choir responding each time with the antiphony, 'His love endures for ever.' Although the repetition might appear wearisome when reading the psalm through, the persistence of God's love is the focal point to which the psalmist relates each element of thanksgiving. It is the Lord's constant love that is the motive power in his creative work; it is his persistent love that has shaped his saving work for his people; it is his unfailing grace that holds us day by day.

God's love for us is 100% reliable. Despite our unfaithfulness, he remains steady and constant. He will not abandon us, but constantly reaches out to draw us back to himself. One of the theses Luther presented at Wittenberg declared: 'God's love does not love that which is worthy of being loved, but it creates that which is worthy of being loved.' Psalm 136 reminds us of the wideness of God's mercy, the persistent and renewing power of his love.

Universal love

One of the regular themes of the psalms is that God's love is not narrowly religious. His love is demonstrated in the world he has made and in his care for each aspect, and each person, within his creation. It is important to realize that God's love is not simply displayed in his actions. He *is* love. It is the essence of his character. But the psalmist encourages us to see that God's actions in the world around are part and parcel of his steadfast love. The natural world expresses the faithfulness and care of a wise creator. It reveals his majesty; it is the theatre of his glory. Whether in things great or small, his providence extends to his entire creation: he made the heavens, he spread out the earth, he set the sun, moon and stars in their place, and he gives food to every creature (verses 5–9, 25).

Jonathan Edwards, the seventeenth-century pastor and theologian, describes his experience of conversion in these words:

> The appearance of everything was altered; there seemed to be, as it were, a calm, sweet cast, or appearance of divine glory, in almost everything. God's excellency, his wisdom, his purity and love, seemed to appear in everything, in the sun, moon and stars; in the clouds and blue sky; in the grass, flowers, trees, in the water and all nature.[2]

Every moment we receive from God's good hand and experience the universal love of the Creator and Father who cares for each of his creatures. Derek Kidner wisely points out that this theme 'invites the Christian not to wrangle over cosmological theories, but to delight in his environment, known to him as no mere mechanism, but a work of steadfast love. No unbeliever has grounds for any such quality of joy.'[3]

Holy love

The Lord is not only the creator of the world; he is also the God of history. He controls not only nature, but also the nations, their rulers and their kings. The psalms therefore review history regularly to encourage us to worship. Here in Psalm 136 we encounter a paradox which often features in discussions of God's love. The psalmist continues to repeat the refrain that God's love has no end. But how does he demonstrate this love? 'To him who struck down the firstborn of Egypt' (verse 10); 'swept Pharaoh and his army into the Red Sea' (verse 15); 'who struck down great kings' (verse 17); 'and killed mighty kings' (verse 18). Do these express God's love? Is there not an impossible juxtaposition of ideas?

The reason we find these verses uncomfortable is that our view of God's love is inadequate. In chapter 2 we noted that some people hold a Santa Claus theology, a sentimental view of God and his love shaped not by biblical revelation but by the distorted perceptions of love in our culture. We saw that the apostle John presented the nature of God as both love and light. The psalmist underlines the same conviction: God's love is a holy love. Once again we see the biblical writers insisting that God's character cannot be compartmentalized.

David Pawson uses a humorous illustration to make the point.

I once knew a family in which the children were never punished. No matter what they did, from smashing windows to painting the cat green, it was excused as childish exuberance or legitimate self-expression. I must admit at times I envied them. But what those parents were offering their children was not love so much as sentimental indulgence. Yet that is what many people think God offers us.[4]

The psalmist declares that we live in a moral universe. God cannot ignore sin or rebellion, and it is a misunderstanding of love to imagine that he should do so. He displays his steadfast love in delivering his people and in judging those who shake their fist at him. The fact that God is love does not make his judgment an empty threat. For sure, God's wrath is his 'strange work', as Luther once called it. Temporary it may be, but it is real nevertheless. And it is one of the reasons some of the psalms 'celebrate' judgment.

Psalm 96 closes with a jubilant celebration on the part of the rivers, trees, mountains and fields, in which we are invited to participate. Why such unrestrained enthusiasm? It joyfully anticipates the coming of the Lord in judgment. 'He will judge the world in righteousness and the peoples in his truth' (verse 13). One day the world will be put to rights. The sorrows and tears of God's people will be over, the ugliness and distortion of a fractured world will be removed, and creation itself will be renewed and restored. Everything will be summed up to find its unity and headship in Jesus himself. The removal of evil and the judgment of the rebellious express his holy love, as the Lord brings order once again to the universe he had made. This is part of the dynamic of truth and love which we are exploring. His holy love combines conviction and compassion in the events of history.

This is true also in the lives of us believers. God's purpose of love is to make us holy, to bring us into conformity with his Son. The writer to the Hebrews reminds us that it is precisely because God loves us that he disciplines us. 'If you are not disciplined . . . then you are illegitimate children and not true sons' (Heb. 12:8). This is never easy for us. But 'if the way is hard, and we think that overmuch discipline is coming our way, then', says David Gooding, 'we must begin to develop the habit of thinking that the Lord must love us very much'.[5]

Helen Lee tells us the story of a warden in a home for deprived and orphaned boys. He brought up his own son with all the others, trying to treat each child equally. One day one of the boys came to him: 'You don't love me as much as your boy, do you?'

Feeling grieved, the warden asked, 'What makes you say that?'

'When he does something naughty, you give him a hiding,' came the reply. 'When I do, you just tell me off a bit.'

That child's measure for love was determined by the severity of the discipline each boy received.

God's love is holy love. He disciplines us so that there will be a 'harvest of righteousness and peace' (Heb. 12:11). There is a goal for which God is preparing his children. Having begun a good work, he will complete it (Phil. 1:6). It will take time, training and discipline, but it is motivated by God's holy and steadfast love for us.

Redeeming love

Deliverance from Egypt was a constant theme in the songs of the Old Testament, and Psalm 136 is no exception. God's love is displayed in his redeeming work: 'he brought Israel out from among them (verse 11); he 'led his people through the desert' (verse 16), 'and gave their land as an inheritance' (verse 21). Israel could rejoice in the overthrow of Pharaoh and his army, and their deliverance from captivity, as expressions of God's persistent redeeming love for them.

The New Testament parallel, of course, is the demonstration of God's redeeming love in the cross of Christ. This is where we see what love means, as John declares in his first letter. It is here at the cross that, as Richard Lovelace puts it, 'the harmony of God's love and justice is perfectly symbolised'.[6]

To those who are tempted to separate God's truth and love, his conviction and his compassion, the cross gives the clearest and most unequivocal answer. God's justice requires propitiation for our sin; God's love offers his Son as the necessary sacrifice. 'This is love: not that we loved God, but that he loved us and sent his Son as an atoning sacrifice for our sins' (1 Jn. 4:10). 'God demonstrates his own love for us in this: While we were still sinners, Christ died for us' (Rom. 5:8). As John Stott summarizes, 'The cross demonstrates with equal vividness both his justice in judging sin and his mercy in justifying the sinner.'[7] God's justice cannot overlook our sin and moral failure; God's love sent Jesus to pay the penalty that we deserved.

It is vital to see this connection if we are to understand the Christian gospel and the nature of love. Sometimes people imply that Jesus' death was 'a great example of love', as if it were no more than a dramatic gesture, or a case of someone so passionately committed to a cause that he was willing to die for it. But to regard the cross as merely an heroic martyrdom, a noble example of courage and dignity, is to miss the force of God's redeeming love.

James Denney gives a good example of what Jesus' death means:

> If I were sitting at the end of a pier on a summer day enjoying the sunshine and the air, and someone came along and jumped in the water and got drowned 'to prove his love for me', I should find it quite unintelligible. I might be much in need of love, but an act in no rational relation to any of my necessities could not prove it. But if I had fallen over the pier and were drowning, and someone sprang into the water, and at the cost of making my fate his own, saved me from death, then I should say, 'Greater love hath no man than this.' I should say it intelligibly because there would be an intelligible relation between the sacrifice which love made and the necessity from which it redeemed.[8]

The love of God is seen in all its fullness at the cross because it was there that Christ suffered for our sins, 'the just for the unjust, that he might bring us to God' (1 Pet. 3:18, AV). Augustine once called the cross a pulpit from which Christ preached God's love to the world. Such love speaks to all men and women, irrespective of time or culture, and to each of us individually. It is a universal, redeeming love that singles out each unique person. When I was a student, a good friend of mine became a Christian through hearing one verse of the Bible read on the radio as he drove his car to work. Knowing his life to be in disarray, he was moved to tears by the words of Paul: 'the Son of God, who loved me and gave himself for me' (Gal. 2:20). It was the force of the personal, individual love of Christ that the Holy Spirit used to open his eyes and heart to God. Paul's emphasis here is the same as John's: love that gives. The Son of God gave himself for *me*. These are the characteristics of love which we are to reflect as God's children – personal love, giving love, love that identifies, love that rescues.

Psalm 136 ends by reminding us of God's contemporary love. He is termed 'the One who remembered us in our low estate' (verse 23). On many occasions God's people were brought low, and each time they experienced God's deliverance. This truth is the same for every singer of the psalm. God's love is as active, real and powerful as ever it was. However low we may feel we have sunk, his love is deep enough. However far we may have wandered from him, his love is wide enough. As Betsie ten Boom was reported to have said in the horror of the Ravensbrück concentration camp, 'There is no pit so deep, that he is not deeper still.' Whatever makes up our lives, whatever burdens we carry, whatever concerns we might have about work, relationships or the future, his love has no end. It remains constant, fresh and powerful. All of our Christian service must flow from this.

In the early autumn of 1994, I was invited to speak at a conference in Stockholm. That weekend, the churches in the city were full. It might have seemed unusual for such a secular European country. But memorial services were being held following a major ferry disaster a few days earlier. The *Estonia* had gone down with the loss of 900 lives. Hardly a family in Sweden was unaffected by the tragedy.

There were two reactions which Christians mentioned to me. Some people were tempted to conclude, as did Voltaire, that either God is not good or he is not powerful. He cannot be both, if such tragedies happen in his world.

But the primary reaction, signalled by packed churches around the country, was one of sadness and humility. Facing overwhelming grief, people did not seem to argue with God so much as turn to him for help, even if they had never done so before. I spoke with one pastor who explained that perhaps they had come to see the emptiness and superficiality of a secular culture, and had been confronted by the fragility of human life. At that moment of bewilderment they had sought the mercy and compassion of God.

It is often when we are up against tragedy that we focus on the priorities in life. Our dependence on wealth, employment, insurance or even family is seen to be inadequate. We come face to face with our finiteness and insecurity, and realize that our lives need a more permanent foundation, our hearts a more settled home.

The Old Testament prophets frequently sought to stress the key priority of life – understanding and knowing the Lord.

> This is what the LORD says:
> 'Let not the wise man boast of his wisdom,
>   or the strong man boast of his strength,
>   or the rich man boast of his riches,
> but let him who boasts boast about this:
>   that he understands and knows me,
>   that I am the LORD, who exercises kindness,
>   justice and righteousness on earth . . .'
>
> *(Je. 9:23–24)*

There is nothing worth relying on if it does not have at its centre the knowledge of God, controlling our aspirations, healing our sorrows, shaping our ambitions and directing our paths. God's goodness in all its variety flows out to us as our knowledge of him deepens, and we discover the depth of his love and faithfulness for us at every point in our lives.

Every aspect of Christian discipleship stems from knowing his love. We shall not be able to obey him, serve him, suffer for him, or even love him, unless we first experience his love flooding our hearts and minds.

> This goal of authentic spirituality {writes Richard Lovelace} is a life which escapes from the closed circle of spiritual self-indulgence, or even self-improvement, to become absorbed in the love of God and other persons. For the essence of spiritual renewal is 'the love of God . . . poured out within our hearts through the Holy Spirit'.[9]

Our capacity to love is entirely the result of his prior love for us and in us.

Christian love

When I was studying in Winchester, I joined with fellow students in various evangelistic programmes in the city. We frequently used a book table as one form of outreach. One January morning a friend of mine manned the book table on the cathedral green. It was a bitterly cold day, but she stayed there for several hours, making contact with passers-by. A member of the Christian student group walked past, and asked her how things were going.

'Fine,' she said, 'but I'm really cold.'

'Never mind,' her friend replied, 'you've got the love of Jesus to keep you warm.'

Later, a second Christian friend came along. 'How are things going?'

'Fine, but I'm really cold.'

'Hang on, then, and I'll get you a hot-water bottle.'

And so she did. Back she came with the promised gift, along with two blankets.

As if retelling one of Jesus' parables, my friend asked me, 'And which of the two do you think was the more spiritual?'

Paul would have had no doubt in the matter. True spirituality, true love, will mean actions, not just words. He explains that God has shown us what his love is like in giving Jesus Christ (Rom. 5:8). Since our life is now 'in Christ', it will be characterized by love. 'Walk in love, as Christ loved us and gave himself for us' (Eph. 5:2, RSV). 'In Christ' and 'in love' coincide.

Our capacity to love, as we have seen, arises from our experience of God's love for us. Paul therefore underlines the priority of genuine love in the Christian life, and most particularly in the Christian community. Anders Nygren comments: 'Love is the circulation of the blood in the body of Christ, through which all its parts and members are related to each other and bound together in oneness.'[10]

In Romans 12, the place of love within Paul's practical list of attitudes and actions establishes its priority. He describes three qualities of the love we are to demonstrate. Our love must be sincere, brotherly and practical.

First, 'love', says Paul, 'must be sincere' (Rom. 12:9). Christian love must be honest, not hypocritical. It can so easily be distorted by mixed motives. We may surround it with a spiritual veneer and describe it with the right language, while all we are doing is trying to cover up our real desires. How can our love be sincere? It will be shaped by a genuine appreciation of spiritual values, Paul says. 'Hate what is evil; cling to what is good.'

If you place a frog in boiling water it will immediately jump out. But if you place it in cold water, and gradually increase the temperature to boiling point, the frog will not jump out. It will boil to death. One of the most acute problems we Christians confront is that, surrounded by so much evil, we become accustomed to it. We keep quiet. We are no longer shocked. We avoid evil, but we do not hate it. We support the good, but we do not fight for it. Paul explains that the motivating force, the power to overcome evil and fight for good, is genuine love. It is the holy love which we have seen celebrated in Psalm 136. We face the special danger of our love being insincere, the worst kind of religious humbug there is. The word 'sincere' here in verse 9 may be translated 'genuine'. Paul uses it also in 2 Corinthians 6:6, where the phrase 'sincere love' is adjacent to 'truthful speech'.

Love must be the overall controlling power in our lives. 'Above all,' Peter exhorts, 'love each other deeply' (1 Pet. 4:8). The priority in our new lifestyle, as those who belong to Christ, is to love 'deeply', or 'fervently'. The word Peter uses has little to do with emotion. Rather, it speaks of the kind of sustained effort shown by an athlete, stretching and straining to complete the event. It is a genuine love that acts, expends itself fully, and gives.

Paul's appeal to the Corinthians stresses the same priority – a genuine love motivating our actions, arising from God's love in Christ towards us. 'The love of Christ leaves us no choice' (2 Cor. 5:14, NEB). Our experience of the sacrificial love of Christ, who gave himself for us, means we have no option. It is a gentle but firm pressure encouraging us to action.

Secondly, Paul exhorts us to 'be devoted to one another in brotherly love' (Rom. 12:10).

I have just watched a television programme which recounted the sad story of Nicholas Geldard, a ten-year-old boy who died after being refused an intensive-care bed in several hospitals. The programme had its political point, of course, but what struck me was the maturity of Nicholas's teenage brother and the obvious warmth of their relationship. When it became clear that Nicholas's young life was over, the doctor in charge indicated to the parents that the life-support systems should be closed down. It was the older brother who took the responsibility. He described how he held his young brother's hand. 'You're the best thing that ever happened to me,' he said. With tears in his eyes he switched off the machine.

I should imagine the two brothers had their disagreements. They were sure to have had fights and arguments as part of the family dynamic. But here was an intimate relationship, a deep bonding, evident in the moving testimony of a teenager bidding farewell to his young brother.

Paul describes Christian love in intimate family terms. It is to be 'brotherly' – tender and affectionate, as one would expect among close family members. This brotherly love arises directly from our relationship with Christ. We shall see in chapter 8 that our unreserved fellowship, our acceptance of one another, is possible because Christ has accepted us (Rom. 15:7). Genuine affection and tender concern for one another are the inevitable outcome of sharing Christ's life. 'God's saving work is at heart a work of love,' comments Marianne Meye Thompson, 'for it brings us into a household of filial and familial relationships, in which Jesus is the foundation and love the mortar.'[11]

Some have compared walking into church with entering a refrigerator. They were referring not to draughty twelfth-century buildings, but to the quality of relationships. Christian love should have a warmth and affection which should mark us out. Such love is not super-spiritual or gushing. Instead, it is wholehearted. The New Testament commands this kind of emotion: 'Be kind and compassionate' (RSV 'tenderhearted'; Eph. 4:32). Often, when relating to other Christians, our hearts are pretty sluggish. But then we need to ask the Lord to forgive our coldness, and to help us respond as the New Testament encourages us: by forgiving from the heart (Mt. 18:35), loving fervently from the heart (1 Pet. 1:22), and loving one another with brotherly affection (Rom. 12:10).

Practical love

Thirdly, we are to 'share with God's people who are in need' (Rom. 12:13). The early Christians were known for their practical care for one another. Their deep commitment to one another is unmistakable in Luke's account of life in this new society. He records that 'all the believers were together and had everything in common. Selling their possessions and goods, they gave to everyone as he had need' (Acts 2:44–45; cf. 4:34–35). As an early Christian writer, Tertullian, described it: 'One in heart and mind, we do not hesitate to share our earthly goods with one another. All things are common among us, except our wives.'

What this means for Christians today needs careful thought. Somehow we need to recover the deep sense of identification and community which they exemplified. Too often we suffer from 'billiard-ball Christianity': we touch one another for the shortest possible time, and in the slightest possible way, and then head off in different directions.

In Romans 12, Paul lists some of the spiritual gifts found within the church. He includes one gift for which Christians rarely pray. He uses the word *charisma* in describing this gift (cf. verse 6), yet it rarely comes to mind when we think of the charismatic gifts about which we read and talk so much. 'If it is [the gift of] contributing to the needs of others, let him give generously' (verse 8). The charismatic gift of generous giving! Whatever our resources, it is a grace-gift to be exercised within the Christian family, and directed in practical ways to meet 'the needs of others'. Ambrose, the fourth-century bishop of Milan, rebuked the church of his day with the observation: 'A slave redeemed at the church's expense is a far better decoration for the Holy Communion table than a golden chalice.'

The reason for such genuine, affectionate, practical love for others is that we are bound together in a common life. 'If one part suffers,' says Paul, 'every part suffers with it; if one part is honoured, every part rejoices with it' (1 Cor. 12:26). We belong to one another because we share the life of Christ. Each individual's pain or joy is felt through the entire fellowship. There should be a brotherly identification with those in need or in spiritual danger: 'Who is weak and I do not feel weak?' (2 Cor. 11:29).

Let me draw this section to a close with one intriguing example of the combined commitment to compassion and conviction which is our theme. Paul's identification with the needs of others led him to urge the Thessalonian believers to 'help the weak' (1 Thes. 5:14). These might have been people who were struggling spiritually; they might have failed in their sexual life; they were the vulnerable in the fellowship. But they were not to be abandoned. They were to be loved; they were to be made to feel that they belonged, and that they had brothers and sisters who supported them and cared for them. The word for 'help' is also translated 'support', and can mean 'cling to'. 'Hold on firmly to the weak.' It is the same word that Paul uses when he encourages church leaders to 'hold firmly to the trustworthy message' (Tit. 1:9). In other words, there is a double commitment for the church: we should have the same determination to hold on to the weak as to hold on to the gospel. They are two clear priorities. Sometimes those known for their tenacity with regard to biblical convictions are not equally known for their compassion for the weak. Our commitment to love must match our commitment to truth.

God's love for us demands a spirit of practical fellowship: not neglecting the needy, not criticizing the weak, not ignoring those with burdens, but responding generously to those in need as fellow members of the family.

The obligations of love

Caring for a handicapped child can stretch parents to the limit. In some cases marriages have not survived. But many of us will know families which have been enriched and strengthened through the presence of a family member with severe physical or mental difficulties. Such families display a depth of mutual commitment, joy and intimacy that others of us do not experience. Talk to the parents of a multi-handicapped child and they will tell you that it is not all sweetness and light. There are days of despair and intense frustration. But there is also a bond of love which drives the family to profound practical care year after year. They understand the *obligations* of love. God has given them a precious gift, and they are to nurture that child with a sense of responsible love. It is rarely sentimental, but it could not be more genuine.

Nearly twenty years ago I made a public promise in a small church in Cumbria: 'to have and to hold from this day forward; for better, for worse; for richer, for poorer; in sickness and in health; to love and to cherish, till death do us part, according to God's holy law'. I am thankful that our marriage has been 'for better' rather than 'for worse', but I made promises which committed me to love's obligations, whatever circumstances we would face.

The fact that love has obligations is a theme rarely explored in Hollywood movies. Our sense of discomfort with the idea arises from the misunderstanding of love to which we have already referred. The romantic notion of 'falling in love' implies a loss of self-control. People describe the feeling as being swept off their feet, falling head over heels, an overpowering emotion unrelated to reason or decision. Presumably that is why *Star Trek*'s Dr Spock cannot place the concept within his logical frame of reference.

In Romans 13, Paul describes our obligations as citizens. We are to submit to the governing authorities which are put there by God himself. Part of that submission for most of us will be the payment of taxes. If we have taxable income we have no choice; our duty is clear. We do not wait for an overpowering emotion before we complete our tax return. We have an obligation to obey the law (Rom. 13:7). Paul goes on to describe a further debt: 'the continuing debt to love one another, for he who loves his fellow-man has fulfilled the law . . . love is the fulfilment of the law' (Rom. 13:8–10). It is important to notice Paul's emphasis. Love is not the end of the law, but its fulfilment. He is not suggesting that we are justified by loving; love is not a way of salvation. But love is our response to God's mercy in saving us. It is expressed through our obedience to his laws, now that we belong to him and live in his kingdom.

James helps us still further. 'If you really keep the royal law found in Scripture, "Love your neighbour as yourself," you are doing right . . . Speak and act as those who are going to be judged by the law that gives freedom' (Jas. 2:8, 12). Like Paul, he insists that love does not replace the law, but fulfils it. There are three points worth noticing about this law of love: the demands it makes, the freedom it brings, and the judgment it entails.

The demands of the law

When Jesus was asked which was the most important commandment, he deliberately linked two Old Testament passages in his reply. 'The most important one', answered Jesus, 'is this: "Hear, O Israel, the Lord our God, the Lord is one. Love the Lord your God with all your heart and with all your soul and with all your mind and with all your strength." The second is this: "Love your neighbour as yourself." There is no commandment greater than these' (Mk. 12:28–31).

Jesus was not downgrading other commandments. He was explaining that all the other laws rested on these two foundations. The first – 'love God' – summarized the first four of the Ten Commandments. The second – 'love your neighbour as yourself – summed up the remaining six. This, James says, is the royal law, the law of God's kingdom. 'Love one another' encapsulates our obligation to obey every demand that Scripture makes concerning our human relationships. Love and law belong together. This is why Paul states that love is happy where truth is (1 Cor. 13:6). If love is to rejoice, truth must be honoured, and God's law obeyed.

The freedom of the law

The royal law of love is wonderfully liberating. It is the 'law that gives freedom' (Jas. 2:12). It frees us from the bondage of self-centred living and enables us to live as God intended.

Sitting on our kitchen work surface at home is an old friend of the family. His name is Julian. He views the world through his small goldfish bowl. He might at times long for greater freedom – to escape the confines of the bowl and jump out on to the floor. But the adventure would not lead to greater freedom. Out of the water, he would soon go the way of all goldfish. But if one of our children were to place Julian in a pond, then he would enjoy greater freedom. He would be living in the environment for which he was made, and would, I hope, have a long and happy life.

True freedom can be found only when we live within the parameters which God the Creator has set. There is no such thing as absolute freedom, freedom without boundaries. We enjoy freedom when we live as God intends us to live.

In his book *Remaking Europe*, Basil Hume seeks to demonstrate why Christian values are essential in today's divided continent. Many European societies face moral uncertainties and confusion. Who decides what is 'good'? Hume refers to an exchange reported in *The Tablet* between a teacher and his students.

A hypothetical moral dilemma faced by a young woman was put before the students. The teacher asked them what she should do. The response was, 'It's her choice.' The teacher insisted, 'Yes. But how should she choose? And on what ground?' The students replied again: 'It's her choice.' In fact the students were making a moral claim. They were saying that there is no value more precious than that a person should be free to determine his or her own good. On this view there can be no moral argument, because each of us creates our own moral rules; and in the name of tolerance we should refrain from moral judgement, as this would be to impose our rules on others. Here is freedom cut loose from its bearings.[12]

It is not true freedom. We are locked into our own world, struggling with subjective choices and imprisoned by the limits of our understanding and experience. It is a mistake to imagine that 'love is all you need'. Love needs definition and focus. It cannot replace all other absolute standards, since it is inadequate as a framework for moral vision and decision-making. Only faithful obedience to God's laws will provide us with true freedom. The royal law of love frees us from the selfishness that is at the heart of our motivation, and releases us to discover God's good purposes for ourselves and for others.

The judgment of the law

Before we conclude, we should not miss the third motivation which James highlights. It would be easy to ignore it. For he calls us to a life of obedient love on the basis of the fact that we shall one day be judged. Again, the ideas might not sit together too comfortably in our minds. Surely, since Christ gave himself for us on the cross, we are free from condemnation? Isn't James getting dangerously close to suggesting that our actions of love are necessary if we are to secure salvation from judgment?

Paul is once again James's ally. He too indicates that Christians will face judgment. He explains to the Corinthians that 'we must all appear before the judgment seat of Christ' (2 Cor. 5:10). This is not a judgment that will determine our ultimate destiny, but a very practical evaluation of how we have lived. The best commentary on this passage is Paul's description in 1 Corinthians 3 of the way in which we are to build for the future. Our lives are safely established on the foundation – Jesus himself. But what kind of building are we erecting on that foundation? What kind of investment are we making? Each of us needs to be careful how we build, because the quality of our work will be tested. On that Day we shall see what will last and what will be burned up. It is a sober reminder that the way we live now matters. Anticipating such judgment saves us from underestimating our moral obligations, and provokes us to live lives of obedient love here and now.

I recently visited Zagreb and met a fine Christian who was

helping the Croatian student movement. He was also running the Christian Information Centre, and an organization called the Peace Circle, seeking to co-ordinate the efforts of various Christian communities at a critical time in Croatia. I commented that this was a demanding set of responsibilities. He replied that this was not the time to have fun; we must use our energies and resources to demonstrate that the Christian faith means something. In the light of the crisis in the former Yugoslav republics, Christians should give themselves wholeheartedly to compassionate service.

I must be careful to avoid misunderstanding. There is an important place in the Christian life for rest and recreation – and for fun too. We are to be more fully human as Christians, not less so. But my friend had a proper seriousness in the light of the challenges in his society. James and Paul are saying something similar: live in loving obedience to God's law, as those who will one day be judged. As Alec Motyer expresses it: 'We shall be delighted with him in that great day. The question is whether he will be delighted with us.'[13]

Truth and love move towards each other

In chapter 3 we referred to the crisis experienced by many of our friends who feel they have lost their bearings. They have no idea where they belong, or how to chart a course for their future. James and Paul have reinforced the importance of God's law in determining how we live our lives. Law and love need each other.

But doesn't it all sound rather cold? As David Field remarks: 'We all know, and secretly abhor, the grim-faced paragon of virtue who strides through life festooned with ribbons of ethical red tape, the moral rule-book poking ostentatiously out of his pocket. Jesus, we are convinced, was never like that.'[14]

God, however, is not calling us merely to keep rules. He is calling us to love him, as a response to his love for us. Obedience will spring from that response of love. Our service is rooted in a relationship with the Father who loves us.

Jesus calls us to follow the way of obedient love. 'If you love me, you will obey what I command . . . If anyone loves me, he will obey my teaching' (Jn. 14:15, 23). As we have seen from John's letters, to love the Lord is to obey him in every detail (*e.g.* 2 Jn. 6). Law and love are partners because they both come from the same source – the Creator, who has ordered his world according to his good and loving purposes for us. 'Law without love becomes legalism,' says Michael Harper, 'and Jesus came to deliver us from it. But love without law becomes soft and sentimental. It lacks depth, direction and content, and Jesus came to deliver us from that also.'[15]

In the last chapter we saw how the biblical understanding of truth involves action: it is truth embodied in believers, and made visible in lives which express Christlikeness. Now we have seen that the biblical understanding of love leads towards that same purpose. Love too means action. It flows from our life in Christ. It is shaped by our assurance of his never-failing love for us, by our understanding of the cross, and by our obedience to his commands. 'The way to prove our love for Christ', writes John Stott, 'is neither by loud protestations of loyalty like Peter, nor by singing sentimental ditties in church, but by obeying his commandments. The test of love is obedience, he said, and the reward of love is a self-revelation of Christ.'[16]

Truth and love move towards each other; they meet in the cross of Christ, and they should combine in committed Christian discipleship. And here is the challenge to the Christian community. How do truth and love affect our handling of disagreements? How do they determine our unity? How do they shape our Christian proclamation and spiritual growth? It is here that we shall encounter the most practical tests of their reality in our lives, and to these themes we now turn.

Notes

1. Michael Harper, *The Love Affair* (Hodder and Stoughton, 1982), p. 66.

2. Jonathan Edwards, quoted in Derek Prime, *Created to Praise* (Hodder and Stoughton, 1981), p. 22.

3. Derek Kidner, *Psalms 73 – 150*, Tyndale Old Testament Commentaries (IVP, 1975), p. 458.

4. David Pawson, *Truth to Tell* (Hodder and Stoughton, 1977), p. 44.

5. David Gooding, *An Unshakeable Kingdom* (IVP, 1989), p. 241.

6. R. F. Lovelace, *Renewal as a Way of Life* (Paternoster, 1985), p. 26.

7. John Stott, *The Cross of Christ* (IVP, 1986), p. 211.

8. James Denney, *The Death of Christ* (Tyndale Press, 1951), p. 103.

9. Lovelace, *Renewal as a Way of Life*, p. 18.

10. Anders Nygren, *Commentary on Romans* (Fortress, 1949), p. 424.

11. Marianne Meye Thompson, *1–3 John*, IVP New Testament Commentaries (IVP, 1992), p. 132.

12. Basil Hume, *Remaking Europe* (SPCK, 1994), p. 26.

13. Alec Motyer, *The Tests of Faith* (IVP, 1970), p. 53.

14. David Field, *Free to do Right* (IVP, 1973), p. 29.

15. Harper, *The Love Affair*, p. 52.

16. John Stott, *The Contemporary Christian* (IVP, 1992), p. 93.

Christian unity

If you have taken a driving test, you probably did not find it a relaxed experience. However many attempts one has, it is hardly stress-free. A friend of mine told me about her ordeal. She explained that she was struggling to select the right gear at that critical moment, the hill-start. She fought with the gear stick while the examiner, clipboard in hand, looked over his glasses wondering how long they would be there. Fortunately for her, he had a ministry of encouragement. 'Don't worry, love,' he said. 'They're all in the same box. All you've got to do is sort them out.'

This sentiment expresses the twin truths of the New Testament when it comes to the subject of Christian unity. First, the Bible is absolutely clear about the unity of all true Christians: we belong to one Father, we are redeemed by the one Lord Jesus Christ, we are indwelt by the one Holy Spirit. We're all in the same box.

At the same time, the New Testament letters, in particular, focus on the question of how that unity must be demonstrated, how the cogs and wheels must engage so that the Christian community can make progress. Few of us can have avoided this painful tension: we believe that Christians are 'all one in Christ', but what happens in the real world is another matter.

In this and the next two chapters we shall consider how truth and love are to shape our life together as Christians. Both qualities are urgently needed if we are to be true to our calling as God's own people. We shall start by looking at the characteristics of Christian unity, particularly as Jesus described it in his high-priestly prayer (Jn. 17). In the next chapter we shall examine some of the practical ways in which Christian fellowship should be informed by conviction and compassion. Then we shall turn to the opportunities as well as the limits of co-operation.

There are two main reasons why it is essential to look at the issue of Christian unity in a book about truth and love. First, unity is founded on a shared understanding and experience of what is true about the Christian faith. We shall see that Christian unity is strengthened, not undermined, by a clearer under-standing of its foundation: we need tough minds. But secondly, unity – and disagreement! – among Christians needs to be expressed within the framework of Christian love. Sometimes, Christians hold to a certain aspect of truth in such a manner that Christian unity is needlessly threatened. Tender hearts can make all the difference.

Yes and no

Some years ago I paid my first visit to Bulgaria. I had not realized that this was the one European country that reversed the usual cultural signals associated with 'yes' and 'no'. Customs are changing now, but at that time, Bulgarians traditionally nodded for 'no', and shook their heads for 'yes'. I wish someone had told me this before I was due to preach. I struggled through my sermon with the congregation shaking their heads; the more passionately I preached, the more vigorously they shook their heads.

Most of us will find it very difficult to nod and say 'no', or shake our head and say 'yes'. It takes a fair effort of the will and, in our culture, we would be sending out two contradictory signals at the same time. But this is exactly the confusion generated when we Christians talk about unity.[1] We affirm a huge 'yes' – that 'we are one in the Spirit' – but at the same time we are furiously shaking our heads: our disagreements, wrangling and tribalism within the Christian community all communicate a very different message.

Non-Christians can hardly be blamed for criticizing what they perceive to be a massive credibility gap between what we say and what we do. As we stressed in chapter 4, truth has to be demonstrated in deeds as well as words. Perhaps at no other point in Christian witness have our inconsistencies been more obvious than in our professions of unity and fellowship. In 1656 Richard Baxter expressed the point in a way that describes our situation nearly 350 years later:

> The public takes notice of all this division and not only derides us, but becomes hardened against all religion. When we try to persuade them, they see so many factions that they do not know which to join – and think it is better not to join any of them. Thus thousands grow in contempt of all religion by our divisions.[2]

In his gospel, John frequently speaks of God's purpose of drawing people together. While he does not use the word 'church', he manifests a deep concern for unity. Jesus' goal is to bring together into one body all the scattered children of God (11:52); he will draw everyone to himself (12:32). He is the one shepherd of the one flock (chapter 10); despite its many branches, there is one true vine to which they are all attached and on which they depend for their life (chapter 15). But perhaps the most famous passage on this theme in John's gospel is Jesus' prayer in the garden, recorded in John 17. Here we find three petitions relating to the unity of believers: 'so that they may be one as we are one' (verses 11, 22); 'that all of them may be one' (verse 21); and 'May they be brought to complete unity' (verse 23).

What are the characteristics of the Christian unity for which Jesus prayed?

A shared experience of life

Twice in these verses Jesus makes a clear connection: the unity among believers is likened to that which exists between Jesus and his Father. Not only that, it is a unity based on a common life, depicted by Jesus as a mutual indwelling: '. . . just as you are in me and I am in you' (verse 21); 'I in them and you in me' (verse 23).

Jesus is describing a supernatural unity. As those who are united to Christ through faith, we now share in a unity identical to that between the Father and the Son. Our life together as Christians is nothing less than a shared participation in the love and communion of the Godhead. Many years ago Francis Schaeffer, speaking about the importance of love and communication in today's world, pointed out how these began – with the members of the Trinity opening the circle and drawing us into their own fellowship of love and unity. Christian community should therefore reflect the mutually supportive love of the Father and the Son. This is the source of love in the Christian life and in Christian unity, as Jesus prayed: 'I have made you known to them, and will continue to make you known in order that *the love you have for me may be in them* and that I myself may be in them' (verse 26).

Christian unity is based on this shared experience of the life of God. We are indwelt by the Spirit, and we are living in union with God himself, dependent on him and experiencing his life and his love. There can be no more secure basis for unity and fellowship among Christians.

John later stresses this in the opening verses of his first letter. Spiritual unity arises from fellowship with the Father and with his Son Jesus Christ (1 Jn. 1:3). Any attempt to construct Christian unity without that fundamental spiritual reality will turn out to be an empty shell. Fellowship with God is the essential prerequisite. Our fellowship with one another arises from the theological realities of the gospel – not simply words we say, but living fellowship with God through what he has achieved in and through the Lord Jesus.

This is well expressed by William Temple:

The way to the union of Christendom does not lie through committee rooms, though there is a task of formulation to be done there. It lies through personal union with the Lord so

deep and real as to be comparable with his union with the
Father.[3]

As with so many aspects of the Christian life, there is clearly a
'now' and a 'not yet'. We are already one because of our union
with Father, Son and Spirit. God's life runs through us as
individual believers and as a new society. Yet at the same time
that unity needs to be brought to perfection, as Jesus prays: 'May
they be brought to complete unity' (verse 23). We know that one
day his prayer will be answered, but meanwhile we need to make
every effort, in our actions and attitudes, to demonstrate the
reality of the life of God. The love which the Father has for the
Son should be expressed within and among us, his people.

This is the first characteristic of Christian unity. If we are
sharing God's life and love, we must be specially careful about our
relationships with fellow Christians, of whatever persuasion or
denomination. In a moving and courageous address to the High
Leigh Conference of Christian Brethren in 1955, Harold St John
argued that we must be cautious before passing judgment on
fellow Christians:

There are those with whom our consciences will not allow us
to walk in church fellowship. I recognise that. There are many
whose consciences will not allow them to walk with us. I
recognise that. But have we ever acknowledged the incalcul-
able debt of gratitude which we owe to the great historic
churches? I think of the Church of Rome, scarlet in her sins,
supreme in her saints and strong in the way she has stood like
a rock in early and medieval history. A score of times she has
saved the framework of the Christian society in days of assault
by the heathen and by heretics.

I recall what we owe to our beloved national Church in this
land, for having kept the faith alive for centuries in the towns
and villages of England. I thank God for our brethren in the
Salvation Army who have reminded us to consider the poor:
and our friends, the Friends, who have poured out their lives,
their wealth, and their sympathies in the service of wretched
refugees in scores of darkened lands. Should not a man lay his

hand upon his mouth before he criticises his brethren? When we pass swift, uninformed, unloving and ungenerous judgements, surely we have forgotten that if we speak evil of them, at the same time we speak evil of the Lord whose name they bear.[4]

There are times when we firmly disagree with others, and when our commitment to biblical truth demands appropriate confrontation. (We shall turn to this in the next chapter.) But as fellow Christians of whatever label, we are identified with the same Lord Jesus. We are indwelt by the same Holy Spirit. We belong to the same Father. As Jesus has affirmed in his prayer, we are part of that trinitarian fellowship, sharing the life and love of God.

A common commitment to truth

John Stott has pointed out[5] that Jesus' prayer in John 17 concerns two groups of people: the apostles, and all who have come to faith subsequently as a result of that apostolic witness. 'I pray also for those who will believe in me through their message.' Christ's prayer is that 'all of them may be one' (verses 20–21). Stott explains:

It is first and foremost a prayer that there may be a historical continuity between the church of the first century and the church of subsequent centuries; that the church's faith may not change but remain recognisably the same; that the church of every age may merit the title 'apostolic' because it is loyal to the teaching of the apostles.[6]

This is a unity founded on our common commitment to that apostolic message. Stott adds to this the fact that Jesus' use of the word 'glory' denotes 'revelation'. 'I have given them the glory that you gave me, that they may be one as we are one' (verse 22). The revelation given to the apostles, and in turn to us, means that our unity as those who have received that witness is strengthened not by ignoring that revelation of God but by welcoming it. Our unity is therefore fostered only by being faithful to the message of the gospel.

This is not easy. But Jesus' prayer shows us that in our desire to strengthen unity among believers, we need both tough minds and tender hearts. Our fellowship is to be founded on his truth and fuelled with his love.

Christian love, as we have seen, comes from our participation in the life of the God who is love. Since this comes only through receiving the truth of the gospel, Christian love can never be increased among us by diminishing the truth which is its foundation. We can know God's love only when we receive his truth.

Evangelicals see themselves as Bible people and gospel people, standing in a tradition which extends back to the New Testament itself. They are defined by two main characteristics: first, the centrality of Scripture as the authoritative, written Word of God, and second, the uniqueness of Christ and the necessity of personal regeneration through his saving work. In summary, their focus is the Bible and the cross. While these might seem theological in character, evangelicals are also committed to the experience of truth. This is implied not only by their preaching of the new birth and their emphasis on evangelism, but also by their desire by God's grace to embody and live out the truth.

There is a range of issues over which evangelicals disagree, but we are united in our stand on the foundation truths of the gospel and in our commitment to the final authority of the Bible. It is these that define our understanding of 'the evangel', the good news which is at the heart of our proclamation of the Christian faith.

The truth, then, is the essential foundation for Christian unity. As Hugh Latimer expressed it in one of his sermons: 'Unity must be according to God's holy word, or else it were better war than peace. We ought never to regard unity so much that we forsake God's word for her sake.'

A powerful witness to Christ

We live in a culture which has become characterized by what R. D. Laing, the radical psychiatrist, called 'social alienation'. At almost every level in society we are witnessing the breakdown of relationships. With fractures running through society, families and individuals, there can be no more important moment to demonstrate Christian unity based on God's love and truth. If in such a world Christians could live out a unity that transcends sexual, economic, social and ethnic divisions, it would be a powerful witness to the transforming work of Christ and relevance of the truth of the gospel.

In Jesus' prayer in John 17, the oneness of his people is linked to the effectiveness of their mission in the world. 'May they be brought to complete unity to let the world know that you sent me' (verse 23); '*so that the world may believe* that you have sent me' (verse 21). It might not be going too far to suggest that this is the primary reason for Jesus' request to the Father – so that men and women will come to believe in who Jesus is and why he came. Bruce Milne lists some of the aspects of disunity that undermine our testimony:

> The biggest barriers to effective evangelism according to the prayer of Jesus are not so much outdated methods, or inadequate presentations of the gospel, as realities like gossip, insensitivity, negative criticism, jealousy, backbiting, an unforgiving spirit, a 'root of bitterness', failure to appreciate others, self-preoccupation, greed, selfishness and every other form of lovelessness. These are the squalid enemies of effective evangelism which render the gospel fruitless and send countless thousands into eternity without a Saviour.[7]

Across Europe and the former USSR we are witnessing the results of the 'new nationalism'. In country after country, particularly but not exclusively in post-communist settings, tribalism is becoming more obviously militant. Ethnic divisions in former Yugoslavia, Hungary, Romania, Bulgaria, former Czechoslovakia, and many Soviet successor states, are tearing families and communities apart. On several occasions, in recent situations of tense ethnic conflict, I have been deeply moved to witness Christians demonstrating genuine reconciliation and unity. I am grateful to God for the experience of standing with believers from Croatia and Serbia who preceded their prayer-time by linking arms and singing:

> There is only one God;
> There is only one King;
> There is only one body;
> That is why we sing:
>> Bind us together, Lord, bind us together,
>> With cords that cannot be broken . . .[8]

A report from the leader of the Burundi Christian student movement described the refusal of student leaders to take sides in the ongoing conflict between Hutus and Tutsis. At the request of the Government, a group of Hutu and Tutsi Christian students visited schools together in order to model reconciliation. On one campus, where the prevailing atmosphere was one of fear and hatred, the group of Christians stood together in unity. They received a message from the university authorities: 'If this university is functioning, it's thanks to this Christian group.' But there is also a cost. In neighbouring Rwanda, most of our IFES movement's board, staff and student leaders suffered in the unrest, several losing their lives in the genocide.

Love of this kind cannot be manufactured. It has nothing to do with being temperamentally compatible or culturally similar. It has everything to do with the miracle of the gospel. It is when we receive the love of God, through accepting the truth, that we are deeply united with fellow believers regardless of their ethnic origin, economic status, social background or Christian denomination. This is where the subject of this book has such profound implications for our day. In a world full of enmity and conflict, such Christian unity can be a powerful witness to the truth of who Jesus is, and how the gospel can reconcile us to God and to one another.

Before coming to our final theme from Jesus' prayer, it is worth examining Paul's stress on unity, which reinforces the emphases we are exploring. His letter to the Ephesians is about the church. It constantly underlines unity in the truth which is maintained and deepened by love. In chapter 2 he uses several illustrations to make his point.

First, we are *God's people*. 'You are no longer foreigners and aliens, but fellow-citizens with God's people' (Eph. 2:19). Our unity arises from our *identity*. We belong to God; we are his. Jesus' mission was to bring home those who were lost, 'you who were once far away' (verse 13). Now we are 'God's chosen people, holy and dearly loved' (Col. 3:12); we are citizens of his kingdom. And that is why, across racial, economic, and ethnic divides, our unity means something. We are not in the first instance English, or Chinese, or Russian. We are his. We belong to him and therefore to one another.

Secondly, Paul builds on the image with a further illustration. We are *God's family*. We are 'members of God's household' (Eph. 2:19). Our unity arises from our *community*. The illustration follows Paul's explanation that through Christ 'we have access to the Father by one Spirit' (verse 18). As family members, we have immediate access to him. Jews and Gentiles are not only brought together as fellow citizens in God's kingdom under God's rule; they are also united as God's children in his family.

While this is probably the most familiar illustration for the Christian church and the nature of our unity, it is vital that we demonstrate its reality. Everywhere there is more and more fracture and disintegration. In some countries of Europe there are growing divisions between the new rich and the socially deprived; ethnic conflict is set to tear families and countries still further apart. And within the church, divisions of all kinds are multiplying. But '[Christ] himself is our peace'; he 'has destroyed the barrier, the dividing wall of hostility' (verse 14). All previous divisions, Paul says, are part of the old humanity. If we are reconciled to God and have come to know him as Father, then we are reconciled to other family members. Christ has broken down the walls and established a brotherhood, a living fellowship, transcending all divisions and uniting us in God's family. This sense of community should motivate us profoundly in all our sustained efforts to maintain 'the unity of the Spirit through the bond of peace' (4:3).

Thirdly, we are *God's temple*. To be a member of God's family means that we are living in the same house as he is. Our unity arises from *God's presence among us*. This picture of 'a holy temple in the Lord' (2:21) is Paul's main metaphor in this passage. It would have been important for the Ephesian Christians. All Jews knew that the temple in Jerusalem was where God dwelt. But, Paul now insists, we are God's dwelling-place! For Gentile Christians in Ephesus, another temple would have come to mind: the massive temple of Artemis. Again, Paul would have pressed the point: the real temple is not in Jerusalem; it is not a stone building dedicated to a pagan goddess in Ephesus: it is we believers.

Paul develops the illustration of the temple by describing its *foundation*. It consists of the apostles and prophets (verse 20), by which he means their teaching. The truth, God's word of revelation, is the foundation. Again we have to underline that we Christians stand or fall by our dependence on the truth of the gospel, the foundation truths which God has revealed. That is the basis of our unity, as we have seen from Jesus' prayer in John 17. Paul goes on to speak of the *cornerstone* – Jesus himself (verse 20). He completes the building, he holds it together, and his presence makes sense of the whole thing. Our Christian community focuses on and depends on the Lord Jesus. It is 'in him' that 'the whole building is joined together' (verse 21). Without him, then, we can have a religious organization or a social club, but no church. Jesus should be at the centre of our life and fellowship. Of course, this temple is still under construction. We are being joined together (verses 21–22) as part of God's building project (1 Cor. 3:9). As Paul stresses in Ephesians 4, it is growing towards maturity as each one plays its part, building itself up *in love*.

God lives in his temple by the Spirit (verse 22). This is why any attempt to destroy the unity of the church is a most serious attack which God will not treat lightly. 'Don't you know that you yourselves are God's temple and that God's Spirit lives in you? If anyone destroys God's temple', Paul says to the Corinthians, 'God will destroy him' (1 Cor. 3:16–17). Too often these verses have been used inappropriately to argue that Christians should look after their bodies, or should not smoke cigarettes. But Paul is talking about Christians as a group: we are collectively God's home, God's dwelling-place. That is why disunity is such a grave matter. Any attempt to destroy that unity provokes a strong reaction from the God whose home is under attack. We belong to God, we belong together, and we are his dwelling-place.

The final illustration Paul gives is in Ephesians 5. We are *Christ's bride*. The imagery is that of being prepared for the wedding-day. In this instance our unity arises from our *destiny*. Paul explains that Christ gave up everything for the church (verse 25). The church exists because of his love. Christ's sacrificial love in going to the cross was for this purpose – to make us fit for an eternity with him. He wants us to become the best that we can be, to become all that God intends, 'holy and blameless', 'without stain or wrinkle or any other blemish' (verses 26–27).

In many countries there is a tradition that the bridegroom should not see the bride's dress until the great day arrives. When Christ returns he will present her to himself in splendour and glory. The bride will be revealed in all her beauty, manifesting God's glory. It is a profound vision. Now, she might look stained, ugly or in rags. On that day, she will be seen for who she is, in her true identity: the bride of Christ made beautiful by Christ himself. He has loved us and given himself for us. He is transforming us, finally to welcome us in the fullness of God's glory.

Both Jesus and Paul have shown us that Christian unity arises from our shared experience of God's life. It is founded on the truth and it begins and ends in the love of God for us and within us.

I began this chapter by highlighting the inconsistencies between what we Christians say about unity and how we live. Where our deeds match our words in demonstrating unity, Jesus will be glorified and the gospel is sure to speed on. In the next two chapters we shall consider how Christians can live together despite their differences and how our witness can be enhanced. We can be full of hope, not only because it is God's life, God's love and God's truth that hold us together, but because of one final aspect of Jesus' prayer which reinforces Paul's reference to the bride in Ephesians 5. It points us to our destiny.

A joyful anticipation of heaven

Father, I want those you have given me to be with me where I am, and to see my glory, the glory you have given me because you loved me before the foundation of the world.   (Jn. 17:24)

In the closing moments of his prayer, Jesus looks beyond history to eternity. It is only in heaven that the unity for which he prays will be brought to perfection. We shall see his glory, and finally and fully experience God's love. It is impossible to imagine, but we shall come to understand the love the Father has for the Son. Together as God's people, from throughout space and time, we shall come to experience that overwhelming love; the circle will finally be completed as Father, Son and Spirit join hands with all the redeemed. Jesus' prayer shows us that God's love is from one eternity to another: 'you loved me before the creation of the world'; 'I want those you have given me to be with me where I am.' We belong to him and one day we shall be with him.

John was given a glimpse of that day in his vision of heaven in Revelation 7. All God's people from throughout the centuries and from around the globe were standing before the throne and the Lamb. They were from every nation, tribe, people and language, and yet there was no confusion of tongues. Babel was a thing of the past, and they sang the praises of God with one voice. The great Puritan preacher, Richard Sibbes, was once described in this way: 'Of this good man let this be written. Heaven was in him before he was in heaven.' All Christians should have that hope in their hearts. It is the vision of God's people, one in heart, one in voice, and one in their worship, finally experiencing 'unity in the faith and in the knowledge of the Son of God' (Eph. 4:13).

There might be many causes for discouragement in our church life, and many temptations to despair as we look at a divided Christendom or a warring congregation. But in such circumstances we should hold on to this characteristic of unity towards which Jesus points us: unity as a joyful anticipation of heaven. We can be sure that Jesus' prayer will be answered.

Notes

1. This illustration came to mind through reading David Cohen and Stephen Gaukroger, *How to Close Down Your Church in a Decade* (Scripture Union, 1992).
2. Richard Baxter, *The Reformed Pastor* (1656: quoted in *ibid.*, p. 27.
3. William Temple, *Readings in St John's Gospel* (Macmillan, 1947), p. 327.
4. F. Roy Coad, *A History of the Brethren Movement* (Paternoster, 1968), p. 226.
5. John Stott, *Christ the Liberator* (Hodder and Stoughton, 1971), pp. 81–88; *idem, The Contemporary Christian* (IVP, 1992), pp. 259–269.
6. Stott, *Christ the Liberator*, p. 82.
7. Bruce Milne, *The Message of John*, The Bible Speaks Today (IVP, 1993), pp. 250–251.
8. From 'Bind us Together' by Bob Gillman, © 1977, Thankyou Music (Kingsway). Used by permission.

Christian differences

After a long and difficult trial, the jury retired to consider its verdict. The hours passed, and the court wondered when a decision might be reached. Eventually the foreman emerged, looking tired and frustrated. He had no word regarding the jury's verdict, but placed an order for eleven cups of coffee and one tea, eleven ham sandwiches and one beef, eleven cream buns and one jam doughnut.

Whenever Christians are in fellowship there are sure to be differences. These might be cultural: some strains in Christian fellowship have to do with social class, background, education, income, manner of dress or lifestyle. Or they might be historical: Christians do not always find it easy to forget past injuries, be they old family feuds, business failures, marriage break-ups, or even hurtful remarks made many years earlier. Classically, of course, they can be doctrinal: disagreement over the nature of spiritual gifts, the role of women in the church, the exact details of the second coming or of the creation of the world.

To give this colourful mix a further dash of excitement, we should add the inevitable diversity of personality types and temperaments. No Christian group or church is without a range of differences with which it must come to terms if it is to survive.

Relatively few churches manage to escape without some pain in the process.

The New Testament makes a point of celebrating diversity, seeing it as a positive asset. Differences are to be expected, and they can enrich our corporate life enormously. But the way in which they are handled can lead either to positive growth and maturity, or to fracture and division. It is clear from Paul's teaching that differing convictions on some issues have to be contained within a fellowship. Paul did not insist that everyone had to line up with his convictions in every detail. For sure, he refused to tolerate error. But he recognized that in many situations Christians might not see eye to eye, and he gave wise advice on handling them. It is because some of us hold strong beliefs without the same strength of compassion that we need to look carefully at his teaching.

First, we shall explore the principles that shape Paul's doctrine of difference; then we shall look at a case study in how to handle relational difficulties.

Living with differences

We have already seen how important unity is within the Christian family, and have noted that agreement with the truth of the gospel is a fundamental ingredient of that unity. Yet whether it is to do with the choice of hymnbook, the colour of the church walls, the style of music in worship, the times of the services, or the use of the baptistry as a sandpit for the mums and toddlers group, there will always be differences, and we must learn to exercise grace in the process of working through them.

In the context of Christian fellowship there are three central ideas which will help us live together with our differences: solidarity in Christ, harmony in the fellowship and clarity about our priorities.

Solidarity: we belong to Christ

The Keswick Convention regularly attracts some 10,000 Christians from a wide variety of churches and traditions. I was recently invited to lead a seminar there on the second coming of Christ. My task was to provide an overview of the subject, including the diverse views held among evangelicals. Traditionally this topic has been an arena for conflict among Christians, with a steady flow of tracts, books and magazine articles adopting various positions, each claiming biblical authority and seeking to provide a test of orthodoxy for other Christians. I was grateful for the fervent prayers of fellow speakers as I put on my flak jacket, anticipating the potential difficulties of leading such a study in the setting of such a broad spectrum of believers and evangelical tribes.

Not only did I emerge unscathed, but there was a remarkable sense of unity and humility. The discussion took place in the Keswick tent with its famous banner above the platform: 'All One in Christ Jesus'. This seemed to have captured the minds and hearts of the group and set the context for our discussion. What tend to be lost in the heated debates concerning differences between Christians are the foundation truths that miraculously create our togetherness. In preparing for the seminar I came across a summary statement by Norman Doughty, which underlines our solidarity as fellow believers:

> Shall we who are relying on the same Redeemer, begotten by the same God, inhabited by the same Spirit, incorporated in the same body, entrusted with the same gospel, assaulted by the same devil, hated by the same world, delivered from the same hell and destined for the same glory – shall we who have so much in common allow ourselves to be divided in heart or service because, just because we are of different minds on this secondary matter? God forbid.[1]

In Romans 14, Paul provides us with a practical 'doctrine of difference' which, properly understood, will help us handle our disagreements with conviction and compassion. It is greatly needed in today's evangelical community.

Paul addresses two groups of Christians, the 'weak' and the 'strong'. The weak objected to buying from the market meat which had been left over from pagan temple sacrifices. They had a particular concern to follow traditions and regulations regarding the sabbath too. In their view, the second group – the strong – were careless and indifferent, quite unspiritual in the way they disregarded what God had commanded. So the weak were committed to upholding God's standards, the more so in the light of the lax and casual attitudes of some of their fellow believers.

The strong, on the other hand, thought that food was food, wherever it came from. And one day was just the same as the next. After all, Christians enjoyed liberty. The weak were in bondage to tradition, and far too rigid in their application of religious regulations. The strong were the *really* spiritual.

I am sure this sounds familiar to most of us. A minister was once asked if he had an active congregation. 'Oh, yes,' he replied, 'they're very active. Half of them are working with me and half of them against me.' It does not take long before groups emerge in the church, clustered around their own emphases or personalities, defining themselves as spiritual over against the others in their fellowship.

In order to help them live together, Paul reminds them first of their solidarity. They belong together *in Christ*. He urges them to accept one another on the basis of their common life. 'Accept him whose faith is weak' (14:1); 'Accept one another, then, just as Christ accepted you' (15:7).

It is the same logic which we have seen both Paul and John use in urging Christians to love one another. This is how God in Christ has acted towards us. Now we should display that same quality to one another. In any dispute with other Christians we must remember that they are members of the family. They are individuals for whom Christ died, as Paul writes: 'If your brother is distressed because of what you eat, you are no longer acting in love. Do not by your eating destroy your brother for whom Christ died' (14:15). They have been accepted unreservedly by God. How can we possibly exclude those whom God has accepted?

Paul presses the point of solidarity still further. The fact that we are all members of God's family means that we are all responsible to the Lord. We shall all stand before God's tribunal.

'You, then, why do you judge your brother? Or why do you look down on your brother? For we will all stand before God's judgment seat' (verse 10). We should not hastily judge others, jumping to conclusions about their lax attitude to the Bible or their rigid spirituality. They are members of the same family (hence Paul's repeated emphasis in verse 10 on 'your brother'). Each of us is responsible to our Master and Lord.

F. F. Bruce once said that there is no sin to which Christians – especially keen Christians – are more prone than that of criticizing others. It can be enormously destructive in a Christian fellowship. But if we recognize that we are redeemed by the one Lord Jesus Christ, we shall want to build bridges rather than lay obstacles between one another.

Should we imagine that we are not guilty of such a critical and judgmental spirit, Paul adds one other word of caution. 'Don't look down on other Christians' (*cf.* 14:3). One of the things I enjoy about my association with the Evangelical Alliance is the humour at council meetings. There is usually plenty of light-hearted banter about our denominational and even our doctrinal differences. It is a mark of fellowship that our trust is not threatened by these friendly exchanges. Humour can often be an important lubricant in situations where Christians disagree. But inappropriate humour can be damaging. Liberated Christians can easily use humour to ridicule their narrower brothers and sisters. It is cruel and insensitive to laugh about what another person regards as sacred. When someone jokes about what I consider to be important, I feel wounded. We should not belittle others when God values them so much.

Paul's first principle in constructing the doctrine of difference is to remind us that we are not isolated individuals, but members of a body. It is the responsibility of each of us to work for the well-being of the whole fellowship. Christians who believe they enjoy freedom must balance their liberty with love for others who might be harmed by their example. Christians who have scruples regarding lifestyle or religious observance must learn not to criticize those who do not share them. We are each members of that one family, indwelt by the same Spirit, accountable to Christ the Lord. We might wish to stand for our convictions. Do so,

Paul commands, with compassion. Demonstrate grace as well as truth as you rejoice in your solidarity in the one body.

Harmony: we belong to one another

It is intriguing to note that Paul's list of the sins of the flesh in Galatians 5:19–21 is heavily weighted towards the divisive sins found within the Christian church. His first list is sexual: immorality, impurity and debauchery. Next, he lists 'occult' sins: idolatry and witchcraft. We would be shocked to discover such sins within the Christian community. But his longest list of sins refers to attitudes that result in the failures which are all too common in our fellowship: 'hatred, discord, jealousy, fits of rage, selfish ambition, dissensions, factions and envy'.

It is a sobering list. These are destructive qualities. By contrast, Romans 14 urges upon us a positive attitude which, instead of destroying our corporate life, will build it up. He appeals for harmony. 'Let us therefore make every effort to do what leads to peace and to mutual edification' (verse 19). His stress is on committed effort, just as he wrote to the Ephesians: 'Make every effort to keep the unity of the Spirit through the bond of peace' (4:3). This will mean creating harmony at every opportunity, working hard at being an influence for good, and developing the much-needed ministry of encouragement. We should not put obstacles in one another's path by insisting on our point of view, but instead 'shoulder the burden of the doubts and qualms of others, and not just go our own sweet way' (Rom. 15:1, J. B. Phillips).

The fact that Paul indicates that it will require effort is noteworthy. Sometimes disagreements between Christians take on a life of their own, gradually developing into a running quarrel. Other members of the church begin to take sides, and a congregation can soon become polarized. The original problem might have been quite trivial, but now it has assumed such proportions that a pastor might find himself engaging in shuttle diplomacy of extraordinary complexity, with all its emotional and spiritual demands. It is therefore worth making the effort early on in order to avoid the snowball effect. Work hard at harmonious attitudes and relationships.

Paul gives an illuminating example in Philippians 4. He appeals to two Christian women, Euodia and Syntyche, who have a disagreement. It is clear that they are both members of the Christian family: their names are in the book of life (verse 3), and they are described as Paul's fellow workers. But they could not get on with each other. There is no clue as to the reason, but we can imagine how matters stood.

Paul stresses the importance of harmony in two ways to these women. First, they must learn to agree (Phil. 4:2). This is the phrase he uses in chapter 2, where he exhorts us to be 'like-minded' (2:2). Learn to agree, he says, because it is this kind of humble-minded surrender that Jesus displayed. Share Jesus' attitude. Paul says the same in Romans 15:3: 'Even Christ did not please himself.' Only this kind of humility can end an argument. And it can be very painful. It might involve asking for the help of others, as was the case here (Phil. 4:3). It will probably mean offering and receiving an apology. It will certainly require an attitude of mind that is geared towards agreement rather than conflict, looking for harmony and resisting the destructive power of discord.

Secondly, Paul appeals for gentleness. 'Let your gentleness be evident to all' (verse 5). The word he uses implies a willingness to give way: not a determination to stand on our rights, to force the issue, but a readiness to go the second mile.

I am, for better or worse, frequently involved in trying to resolve conflict. Sometimes the clashes are between Christians from different cultures, with differing expectations of how Christian work should be carried out; sometimes they arise from the diverse theological convictions which inevitably come to the fore when working across Christian denominations; sometimes they are to do with individual style and personality. In the heat of the debate I notice a tendency in myself as much as in others for my own attitudes to harden; as others express their position more forcefully, I move slightly further away from possible compromise and towards a more extreme position. It might be more entrenched than initially I would have wished to adopt, but somehow the atmosphere pushes me further away from the opposing view.

Gentleness results from the Spirit's ministry in our lives. It is the fruit of genuine love for a fellow member of the family. It defuses conflict and breathes a spirit of reconciliation.

Harmony is essential if we want to give authentic evidence of our own reconciliation with God. It is at the heart of the gospel of truth and love. It arises from our relationship with Christ: 'agree with each other *in the Lord*' (verse 2).

Priority: be clear about what matters

Some years ago I was in touch with a group of Christians seeking to witness to Christ on a large housing estate. Their church building was surrounded by rows of council houses, a strategic location which made it ideal for ministering to a range of needy people. A youth club was started, with teenagers using the facility for sport, and local believers building bridges of friendship. Within a few weeks I heard that the work had been closed down. The reason was disagreement among the church leaders over one small issue: whether girls coming to the youth club should be allowed to enter the building wearing trousers.

For those with a vision for evangelism on the estate and a commitment to compassionate care for the young people concerned, such a disagreement, with its sad consequence, must have been heartbreaking. Yet the story could be multiplied many times over in one form or another. It is one of the prime strategies of the devil to divert Christians from the work of God by distracting them with secondary matters, leading them into time-consuming debates about trivia.

In Paul's doctrine of difference, the third and most critical emphasis is this: *be clear about what matters*. Determine your priorities. 'For the kingdom of God is not a matter of eating and drinking, but of righteousness, peace and joy in the Holy Spirit' (Rom. 14:17). He says much the same in 1 Corinthians 4:20: 'The kingdom of God is not a matter of talk but of power.' Life in God's kingdom cannot be reduced to what we should eat and drink, what we should wear, what church furniture we should buy, or what time our services should be. The real priority is that Christians should display righteousness, peace and joy, and that the gospel should speed on and triumph.

The story is told of Admiral Nelson, who, shortly before the Battle of Trafalgar, heard that Admiral Collingwood was not on good terms with Captain Rotherham of another ship within his fleet. So he called them together. Joining their hands, he pointed to the French ships on the horizon and said, 'Yonder is the enemy.' They returned to their ships to work side by side in the battle.

It is all too easy for our priorities to become distorted. We fight each other rather than the enemy; we give our energies to internal wrangling rather than to the desperate needs of a broken world. Seek first the kingdom, Jesus urged. There is no better way to confront the potentially divisive issues in our fellowships than by asking: what is it that really matters? Paul's key priority is that our eyes should be focused on Christ and our goal should be God's glory. 'May the God who gives endurance and encouragement give you a spirit of unity among yourselves as you follow Christ Jesus, so that with one heart and mouth you may glorify the God and Father of our Lord Jesus Christ' (Rom. 16:5–6).

Occasionally disagreements surface over what are perceived to be priority areas. These are often demanding ethical and pastoral matters, such as homosexuality, divorce and remarriage, or abortion; but they can be theological issues such as the nature of hell, charismatic gifts, and the baptism in the Spirit. How do we respond when confronting disagreement in areas which shape our lives and congregations so decisively, and which can be very emotionally loaded?

Return to foundations

First, we have to be clear about the priorities of the gospel. It is relatively easy for some of us to convert a minor issue into a principle of central importance, and in so doing to hold everyone else to ransom. A very important starting-point is to ask if this issue is crucial to what it means to be a Christian. Is it part of the biblical meaning of the gospel? This is important because of the growing tendency in some countries for people to define orthodoxy according to secondary issues, not just primary ones. In some circles,

. . . a person can only be considered an evangelical if she or he believes in a free-market economy, is an advocate of the nuclear deterrent, is opposed to most forms of biomedical technology, and/or is a scientific creationist, and a strident anti-abortionist. The question is whether these issues should be made *theological* watersheds.[2]

A good example of the need for clear definition of the foundations is found in Acts 15, where Luke records two situations of disagreement in the church. This chapter is frequently cited as an example of how to handle differences, and rightly so. The first example of 'sharp dispute' (verse 2) arose over the circumcision of Gentile converts. Was it necessary or not? One group, the Judaizers, insisted that it was essential: 'Unless you are circumcised, you cannot be saved' (verse 1). Clearly, this was no secondary issue, for it dealt with the heart of the Christian message: how is a person saved?

The matter was therefore referred to the apostles in Jerusalem, who allowed the believers belonging to the party of the Pharisees to argue their case. Then, in turn, the case against circumcision was put. Finally, James presented a scriptural response and condemned any attempt to impose Jewish ritual law. 'We should not make it difficult for the Gentiles who are turning to God' (verse 19). Since it was a question of foundation truth – how people become Christians – it was debated clearly, Scripture was seen as the final authority, and a decision was made which then shaped the life and activity of the church.

But at the end of chapter 15 a second disagreement surfaces. Here it was to do with who should serve on the missionary team. Some thought John Mark was suitable, while others did not. The reactions of Barnabas and Paul, who took opposing positions, in some sense reflect their differing temperaments and their different perspectives on working relationships. But in this instance the matter was not referred to Jerusalem. Time was not wasted trying to negotiate a compromise solution. They decided to set up two teams and to press on with the missionary challenge. The disagreement remained, but it did not stand in the way of the advance of the gospel. The first example in Acts 15 revolved around the foundation truth of the gospel, and so demanded resolution; the second concerned working practice, and differences could be tolerated.

Clarity regarding these priorities is vital. Assessing priorities is specially demanding in pastoral situations, where sometimes tough love is needed. Stephen Travis, writing about issues of judgment, makes the point:

> Whilst in the short term it may sometimes seem wisest to soft-pedal an unpleasant truth, this only leads to confusion in the long run. Truth itself is more important than pastoral expediency. A major reason why many people are in doubt about their relationship to God is that for many years they have not been taught clearly the message of judgment and salvation from judgment.[3]

How then are we to determine what is primary and what is secondary? As we have seen, it is a matter of foundation truth: is the issue at the heart of the gospel? Is it related to the question of how a person comes to saving faith? As Bob Horn expresses it: 'These beliefs have saved lives, changed lives and cost lives.'[4] They are the core Christian beliefs, listed by many churches and Christian organizations in the form of a statement of fundamental truths.

It becomes necessary, then, to ask whether the issue under discussion is peripheral or central. Am I expressing allegiance to a view more associated with my particular denomination or personal experience, or is it something of ultimate importance to all Christians? To divide our concerns into central and peripheral is artificial in the sense that all truth is God's truth. Something 'peripheral' is not thereby defined as something unimportant. But clearly it should not be elevated in our discussions or disagreements to the extent that it displaces or overshadows something primary.

Paul saw the gospel as centring on Jesus Christ and what God has done through him. The primary issues in his teaching focus around the *identity of Christ* – his status as the Son of God and his genuine humanity; the *work of Christ* – his death for our sins and thus the centrality of the cross, his burial, resurrection and future coming in judgment; and then how these truths relate to *our salvation* – our justification by faith in Christ and his work. Paul held tenaciously to these core truths of the gospel. Similarly, our convictions should focus around our understanding of the Scriptures as the inspired Word of God; our faith should be centred on the person and atoning work of Christ; and our stress should be on the vital need of repentance and faith for personal conversion, displayed through active obedience to the truth in Christian witness and service in the world.

We shall proclaim these certainties without compromise, and make known these primary truths with passion and gentleness (1 Pet. 3:15). Naturally, we might hold our convictions on secondary issues with considerable firmness too. But disagreement on these points (which are peripheral, not central to the gospel) should never close the door on fellowship with other believers. We should never lose a sense of respect for the other person in our dialogue, and we should be able to pray with them, enjoy fellowship with them, and disagree courteously.

Follow wise procedures

If our first response to disagreement is to return to the foundations, the second is this: we need to handle the debate wisely. (Whether issues are of central importance or not, *how* we disagree is important.) I offer three simple guidelines.

Our style. Learning to debate on the basis of respect for the other person and for his or her position is an important discipline in serious disagreement. It is all too easy to imagine that our opponent lacks integrity. We shall make progress in our discussion as we listen, and ideally as we discuss face to face. We shall discover that there is a real human being opposite us, with real feelings and genuine faith. In turn we shall learn to respond with grace and humility.

Our motives. The New Testament demonstrates that we need a *twofold* motivation in our debate: a concern to uphold the truth, but also (and easily forgotten) a concern for the welfare of the other person. Paul stresses that we should be gentle with those who oppose us (2 Tim. 2:24). We should avoid any style of communication that destroys others or fails to build them up (Eph. 4:29). Fights and quarrels in the Christian community are governed by selfish desires, not a genuine concern for truth (Jas. 3:9ff.). 'To "speak the truth in love" does not mean hurtful "frankness" with a manipulative veneer,' writes Anthony Thiselton, 'but grounds truthful speech in a stable attitude of respect and concern for the other.'[5]

Our core commitments. Where we confront demanding pastoral issues, then the force of truth and love *together* represents the only way forward. Anyone in pastoral ministry needs a tough mind and a tender heart. This will not necessarily remove the disagreement or resolve the pastoral dilemma. But it will set the tone for our attempts at resolution, provide the boundaries for our negotiation, and demonstrate that we are serving 'that great Shepherd of the sheep' (Heb. 13:20). In a wise article on homosexuality, Christopher Townsend has written:

> The Christian community must respond to the issue of homosexuality and homophile people in a way that combines love and truth, compassion and biblical integrity. There are homosexual people outside our churches or struggling within them because as Christians we have not yet learned to love as we should. Meanwhile, the debate among Christians about homosexuality is, implicitly, a debate about how to do theology . . . Love and truth are not in the end isolated from, or opposed to, one another. The church will only be able to love homosexual people to the full if we have, along with more tender hearts, a firm grasp on the searching insights and transforming power of Christian truth.[6]

Overcoming relational problems: a case study from Philemon

Christian relationships are usually the most rigorous testing-ground for the qualities of truth and love which we are exploring. Much of my work is associated with the development of short-term cross-cultural teams across Europe and the former USSR. At the time of writing, nearly 200 people from some fifteen different countries and as many Christian traditions are working together in forty cities, united in their commitment to the gospel and their vision to see the word of the Lord triumph. It is a wonderful example of God's many-coloured grace at work. But it has its moments. Inevitably, when throwing together young graduates from such diverse backgrounds, and placing them in a foreign culture with its stresses and strains, there are plenty of opportunities for friction.

Many Christian missions report that this represents the greatest challenge to new missionaries: not the uncomfortable climate, the unfamiliar diet, the challenges of language, the cultural disorientation, or even resistance to the gospel in the host culture, but getting on with fellow Christians at the mission station. The same is true in any context where Christians are working together. We struggle with interpersonal conflict, personality clashes, and selfish behaviour patterns. Full-time missionaries are not immune.

We have seen the importance of handling differences according to biblical priorities. How can we reflect the twin qualities of grace and truth in seeking to overcome problems in relationships and strengthen Christian fellowship? We shall find some important clues in the story of Philemon.

The church of Philemon's day knew a great deal about barriers in society. Men and women, slave and free, rich and poor, Jew and Gentile – each was a separate class, surrounded by dividing walls. The gospel was therefore a radical message in the first century. The walls came tumbling down: 'Here there is no Greek or Jew, circumcised or uncircumcised, barbarian, Scythian, slave or free, but Christ is all, and is in all' (Col. 3:11). In this new community, distinctions based on race, nationality, education and social position were unimportant. It was whether a person had Christ that mattered. This truth was clearly demonstrated in Paul's short letter to Philemon. It is a moving appeal which has much to say about how we can approach relationships in a manner which combines conviction and compassion, truth and love.

The story is simple. Onesimus the slave originally belonged to Paul's friend Philemon. As far as we can tell, he was not the best of slaves ('useless' is the word in verse 11 of Paul's letter), and in the end he ran away from Philemon, probably stealing from him as he went out of the door (verse 18). He eventually arrived in Rome where, in fear of his life, he met Paul and responded to the gospel. Now that he was a fellow believer and brother, Paul decided to write to Philemon and reintroduce him to Onesimus, now not just as a slave, but as a brother in Christ. It is a story about overcoming barriers, and about radically different relationships in the Christian family. Let me highlight four keys to resolving the relational problems between Onesimus and Philemon.

Centred on Christ

First, Onesimus is to be welcomed back 'no longer as a slave, but better than a slave, as a dear brother. He is very dear to me,' Paul says, 'but even dearer to you, both as a man and as a brother in the Lord' (verse 16). The old relationship of master and slave is absorbed into the new relationship of brothers in the family. This is the heart of Paul's appeal, particularly moving since both Onesimus and Philemon came to faith through Paul's witness (verses 10, 19).

As we have seen already, the simple rule in the Christian family is this: all relationships are to be viewed from the standpoint of Christ. We may have different temperaments, backgrounds, economic status or nationality, but the closest relationship of all overcomes all such barriers: we are in Christ, brothers and sisters in a fellowship arising from our unity in him.

Motivated by love

Secondly, the whole letter breathes an atmosphere of Christian love. Paul is writing to someone who was known for his loving actions: 'I hear about your faith in the Lord Jesus and your love for all the saints' (verse 5); 'Your love has given me great joy and encouragement' (verse 7). For his part, Paul deliberately stresses that he is not insisting on a particular action by virtue of his apostolic authority. Instead, 'I appeal to you on the basis of love' (verse 9).

Philemon was probably a member of the Colossian church, and Paul's letter to the Colossians has the same pattern of thought: the gospel of truth should be evident in a life of love. He speaks of 'the faith and love that . . . you . . . heard about in the word of truth' (Col. 1:5). To live as a Christian means to become more completely like Christ, to reflect the image of the God who is love. It will thus mean exhibiting the qualities of love which we have already explored – self-giving, self-sacrificial care for others. Sometimes the tone and style of our relationships revolve around our position, status or feelings. Sometimes we might appeal to the way we were made, our temperament, or the way we were brought up. We cannot change how we react to others, we say.

But Paul urges Philemon not to stand on his rights, and not to view his relationships from a secular perspective, but instead to receive a brother in Christ on the basis of the love he has heard about in the word of truth, the love he has experienced for himself in the welcome Christ has given him.

One aspect of love which shines out in the short letter is the ability to identify with someone. It is an impressive feature of Paul's relationship with Onesimus. We can see the sequence clearly: Onesimus is 'my son' (verse 10), 'my very heart' (verse 12), and 'very dear to me' (verse 16); he is to be welcomed 'as you would welcome me' (verse 17). Even his debts were to be charged to Paul's account (verse 18). By treating Onesimus generously, Philemon will 'refresh my heart in Christ' (verse 20).

Philemon must have got the point. How could he treat Onesimus as less than human, or lower in status than himself, when this new Christian meant so much to Paul? It is an important example, which shows us that Paul had a tender heart as well as a tough mind. He is often misrepresented or misjudged – Paul the theologian, hard-headed, dogmatic, dispassionate, cold. But Paul cared deeply for people. He formed strong friendships. A runaway slave found in the great apostle someone who turned out to be closer than a brother, who identified with his needs and became a true friend.

Our personalities vary. Some of us are more demonstrative in relationships, while others are naturally more reserved. But the ability to identify with and care for one another is an essential element of Christian relationships. It arises from our shared life in Christ, and means we shall work hard to understand one another, to give time to strengthening our friendships and to empathize with one another's needs. And it is a key to overcoming difficulties in our relationships. Notice that Paul did not dodge the truth about the failings of Onesimus. He did not ignore the slave's crimes, or forget the outstanding debt – which he offered to pay himself (verse 19). In this he echoed the gospel, the way in which God has acted towards us. Luther once said that all of us are Onesimuses. Love is willing to pay a price to set relationships straight.

Learning to identify is at the heart of good relationships. I notice within myself how quickly I can become impatient with those who do not see eye to eye with me, or whose way of doing things is different. But if I give time to understanding who they are, to learning more about what motivates them and what shapes their life and their responses, and to identifying with some of their struggles, my impatience dissipates. I perceive my arrogance for what it is. I learn to lay aside some of my own expectations, and instead become aware of the needs of others. This leads to the third key in the story of Philemon.

Willing to forgive

Onesimus was guilty of one of the most serious offences in the first century. He could expect a severe punishment according to ancient law, even the death penalty. Paul's appeal needs to be seen in that context. He is asking Philemon not just to forgive Onesimus but to accept him, and to welcome him as a brother (verses 16–17). We are back to the simple but demanding principle found throughout the New Testament: act towards others as God has acted towards you; forgive as you have been forgiven (Mt. 6:5–15; Eph. 4:31–32). True forgiveness aims to treat the other person as we ourselves would wish to be treated. Sometimes we treasure the past failings of others. We store them where they can be immediately recalled. They surface every time we meet the person, every time we have another confrontation. We can never live at peace until we have learned to give the past to God.

Forgiveness refuses to allow the wrong to stand in the way of restoring the relationship. It moves beyond retaliation, bitterness and resentment, and opens the door to building something new. Forgiveness in relationships becomes redemptive, but it is a costly process. Grace is never cheap, whether in its most profound expression in the cross of Christ, or in its reflection in our willingness to demonstrate forgiving love to those who have hurt us.

When I first arrived to work full time in a congregation, one of my initial duties was to visit a family which had been pulled apart through internal feuding. The impact of the broken relationships was profound, almost destroying family members in the process and, inevitably, affecting relationships within the church at large. What became clear as the story unravelled was that the feuding had a history, and looked as though it had a future too. Both husband and wife blamed their parents, who were known for their sharp disagreements. And now the children, despite the appeals of those of us charged with the pastoral duty to try and make peace, refused to close the door on the past. It seemed to be in their blood: they would never speak to their father again, never acknowledge his letters or birthday gifts. It would roll forward to a third and fourth generation.

The fallout from such a breakdown in relationships is catastrophic, and its impact is heartbreaking. Only one thing will break the cycle: God's forgiving love. It has been an enormous encouragement to me to witness this in action. The husband involved in the sad story I have just related discovered and demonstrated the grace of forgiveness. He still carries the scars and feels the pain, but by God's power he has broken the evil cycle of bitterness and vindictiveness. The truths expressed by Gordon Bridger and David Atkinson are apt:

We need to hear from God, from others, from within our own hearts, that we can be forgiven and we need to learn to forgive. The past cannot be undone, but its wound can be healed, and there is no need for our sins to accumulate for ever against us. Guilt can be taken away. Wrong directions can be changed, not by pretending that everything was all right really, because it wasn't, but by building on the past creatively for the future. Not by living with the burdensome law of retaliation, 'You owe me, so you must pay', but by walking again in the fresh air of grace.[7]

In the case of Philemon, he was being asked to go one step further. By God's grace we might be able to forgive people, but do they not need to see something more – our kindness towards them? Paul encouraged Philemon not just to forgive Onesimus grudgingly in order to please the apostle. The robbed slave-owner was asked to give the runaway a royal welcome.

The love that has the power to forgive is desperately needed in our homes, our churches and our society. It is the love God showed his people Israel, the love of a faithful husband towards his adulterous wife. It is the forgiving love which stretches out to the wounded or the disobedient, and speaks the same language as the Lord to his unfaithful people: 'I will heal their waywardness and love them freely' (Ho. 14:4).

Ready to confront

The short letter of Philemon is gentle but bold. It is a great piece of writing. Paul has composed his appeal with enormous tact and care. But there is nothing awkward about it. It is motivated by love, but its frankness and directness are refreshing. Here lies the fourth key in this story of reconciliation. Paul is up front with his bold request. He is firm but also personal. 'If you consider me a partner . . .' Paul says (verse 17), using a word related to the well-known one for 'fellowship', *koinōnia*. They share in the work of the gospel; they have so much in common. So he can talk straight. He appeals to Philemon to sort this relationship out. Be generous and forgiving, he urges.

Many Christians cannot do this. We never say what we feel to people, or confront them in a godly manner. We tell others, perhaps, but we could never express our thoughts to the person concerned. When Christians disagree, or when there is a need to correct, exhort or even rebuke, we lose our nerve. We remain silent, or we talk to someone else. But the ability to confront is a major element in right relationships. It is one of the most important practical areas where conviction and compassion need to work together.

Matthew records some straightforward teaching of Jesus in this regard. If you remember that another Christian has something against you, he says, do something about it. Take the initiative and go to the person; take practical action towards reconciliation if you realize you have caused offence (Mt. 5:23). If your brother has offended you, an equally clear procedure is spelt out in Matthew 18:15–17. It means face-to-face meeting, one-to-one discussion. It might need to involve others eventually, but ideally it should be dealt with by the two of you. And again the goal is reconciliation. Sometimes Christians will not respond to our request even to meet to discuss things; this is sad, but it happens. They feel threatened, or vulnerable, or uncomfortable. In that case, as Jesus indicates, we are to bring in other believers. We are to try to create an atmosphere which will allow each person to express himself or herself openly, and to confront the issues honestly.

It would be wonderful if Christians agreed never to criticize one another publicly – whether writing to the press, talking behind their backs, or sharing their point of view ('in love') at a church meeting – until we had first met face to face to talk it through. In his third letter, John describes his difficulty with Diotrephes, who loved to take the lead and to gossip maliciously about other Christians, and even expelled other Christians from the church for no good reason. 'I have much to write to you,' John says to the believers, 'but I do not want to do so with pen and ink. I hope to see you soon, and we will talk face to face' (3 Jn. 13–14). Meeting in this way, as Jesus commanded, helps us to view the issue in perspective. It clears the air and frequently lowers the temperature in the debate. The words we use face to face are usually more measured and less aggressive. And as we have seen, with the help of another Christian as third party we can often find our way to overcoming the problem. Godly confrontation needs to happen far more frequently than it does, and once again it will take its shape from the twin qualities of conviction and compassion.

Paul's gentleness alongside his boldness indicates his tender heart as well as his tough mind. His pastoral style reflects his passionate concern that truth and love should work as partners. Where someone rejects the clear teaching of the Bible, Paul implies that we need both conviction and brotherly love.

> If anyone does not obey our instructions in this letter, take special note of him. Do not associate with him, in order that he may feel ashamed. Yet do not regard him as an enemy, but warn him as a brother. *(2 Thes. 3:14–15)*

What do we do when we see someone failing? 'If someone is caught in a sin, you who are spiritual should restore him *gently*.' When the sin of another Christian becomes known in our fellowship, gentleness is not always the first and most obvious feature of our response. But it arises from a sense of identification and humility. 'Watch yourself', Paul continues, 'or you also may be tempted. Carry each other's burdens, and in this way you will fulfil the law of Christ' (Gal. 6:1–2). We are all made of the same stuff, and we all need God's grace if we are to avoid the pitfalls of our fallen brother or sister. And what is the 'law of Christ'? It is the law of love. It is with truth as our guide and compassion as our motivation that we should seek to restore the person who has failed.

God's love is uncompromising. He will not tolerate the intolerable; his love never compromises his holiness. But his mercy stands alongside his judgment; his grace redeems and restores the sinful and broken. And it is this unique blend of truth and love which should shape relationships among Christians. If this were to happen, the witness of the Christian community would have renewed integrity and power in the fractured world where God had placed us.

Notes

1. Quoted in David Pawson, *When Jesus Returns* (Hodder and Stoughton, 1995), pp. xi–xii.
2. D. Gareth Jones, *Coping with Controversy* (Visjon Publications, New Zealand, 1994), p. 108.

3. Stephen Travis, *I Believe in the Second Coming of Jesus* (Hodder and Stoughton, 1982), p. 203.

4. Robert M. Horn, *Ultimate Realities* (IVP, 1995), p. 7.

5. Anthony Thiselton, *Interpreting God and the Postmodern Self* (T. and T. Clark, 1996), p. 37.

6. Christopher Townsend, 'Homosexuality; Finding the Way of Truth and Love', *Cambridge Papers* 3/2 (June 1994), p. 4.

7. Donald Bridger and David Atkinson, *Counselling in Context* (HarperCollins, 1994), p. 208.

Christian co-operation

There has always been mutual hostility between the members of the 'Pure and Simple Faith Baptist Movement' and the rival sect in town, 'The Only True Original Baptist Church of the New Testament'. The elders of the respective chapels never spoke to each other, but on one occasion an elder who had dangerously moderate leanings decided to try and start a conversation. He nodded at an elder from 'The Only True Original' sect and remarked, 'I passed your chapel the other day.' 'Thanks,' came back the reply, 'I appreciate it.'[1]

It is a surprising paradox of European Christianity that in the countries where evangelicals are the weakest numerically, they can sometimes be the most fragmented. I frequently visit Christians in Eastern Europe and the Soviet successor states. For many years they have been courageous in their stand for the truth of the Christian faith, ready to face imprisonment or the loss of job and family rather than deny their faith in Christ.

The story of their bravery and commitment during this century has yet to be fully told. But one of the consequences of confronting hostility over such an extended period is a tendency towards isolationism. Let me be clear that I do not write this with a judgmental spirit. I come from an evangelical community which has never faced the demands of persecution, but which has succumbed to compromise and indifference in an atmosphere of materialism and secularism. But when true Christians have been under pressure, either from nominal Christianity or from communism, it has been understandable that they have sometimes erected their defences, pulled up the drawbridge, and consolidated within their own communities.

The result in today's new Europe has been a ghetto mentality. The Baptists are suspicious of the Pentecostals down the road; the Lutherans are uneasy about the Free Churches; the Brethren are shocked by the excesses of the independent charismatic fellowships. Many evangelical churches in Europe, committed to the foundation truths of the Bible and the cross (as we stressed in chapter 6), are nevertheless deeply uncertain about any cause which seeks to unite evangelicals across the denominations. At a time when opportunities for Christian witness are so considerable at almost every level of European society, the lack of evangelical co-operation is nothing short of a tragedy.

In describing the nature of Christian fellowship in the last two chapters, we have identified several key features.

First, *unity is a priority.* Jesus prayed for this and died for this. It is distressing whenever God's people are divided and their witness is hampered. Division within the Christian family is deeply debilitating; it paralyses us and diverts our energies. It fails to demonstrate the reconciling power of the gospel and strikes at the heart of our integrity as Christ's disciples.

Secondly, *unity is based on truth.* We have seen that the foundation truths of the gospel matter. Any attempt to foster Christian unity without proper regard for a shared commitment to the essentials of the gospel (particularly our understanding of Christ and how we receive salvation) is bound to produce a superficial and flawed unity, not the unity which the Bible recognizes.

Thirdly, *we need a doctrine of difference.* Where Christians are united on the fundamentals of the gospel, mature fellowship will allow for differences over secondary matters. We have explored Paul's teaching in Romans 14 – 15, in which he demonstrates that commitment to solidarity, harmony and priority will help us live together despite our differing perspectives on church order, spiritual gifts, the details of the second coming, and much else.

Fourthly, *compassion should always accompany conviction.* Whether it is godly confrontation in pastoral care, handling disagreements in relationships, or formulating our theological convictions over against other Christian traditions, love and truth are essential partners.

There are therefore three issues which emerge from these conclusions, which we shall try to address in this chapter. First, Christian co-operation is a clear priority for all of us who desire to follow Christ's teaching and example. Secondly, such co-operation is both inclusive and exclusive: it has wide opportunities but it also has its limits, as defined by the gospel. Thirdly, the *manner* in which we develop such partnerships or, even more significantly, decide against such co-operation, is crucial. Our behaviour towards others will not only be defined by our convictions; it will be shaped by our compassion. In this vital area we shall need tough minds and tender hearts.

Of first importance

In making our decisions regarding co-operation with other Christians, we must first ask one another the questions we explored in chapter 6: are we committed to the 'evangel'? As we saw in the case of handling differences in Christian fellowship, we need to establish what is essential or primary, and what can safely be viewed as secondary – a doctrine over which disagreement will not be critical to the cause of the gospel.

John's letters have helped us throughout this book. His combination of truth, love and obedience is a model exposition of our central theme. In 2 John he writes about the special danger of false teachers in the church. In the space of a handful of verses John repeatedly affirms the importance of both truth and love.

The believers to whom he is writing, whom he 'loves in the truth', are described as those in whom the truth is living. His greeting specifically reminds them that grace, mercy and peace 'will be with us in truth and love' (verse 3). While he rejoices that they are 'walking in the truth', he also reminds them of the

command to 'walk in love' (verses 4, 6). He longs to see all
believers combine these two qualities. Yet his letter is surpris-
ingly blunt when it comes to advice about the false teachers –
those who run ahead and do not continue in the teaching of
Christ (verse 9). He describes them as deceivers, and recommends
decisive action: 'do not take [them] into your house or welcome
[them]'.

In short, John urges that we reject those who 'do not
acknowledge Jesus Christ as coming in the flesh' (verse 7). This
phrase summarizes who Jesus is and what he has done for our
salvation. Already in verse 3, John has underlined that God has
revealed himself in Christ and fulfilled his purposes in him. If this
is denied, John says, then the essentials of the gospel have been
betrayed; the false teacher must not be tolerated. This, remember,
was written in the context of several encouragements to 'walk in
love'.

The same challenge to guard the essentials remains today. As
Marianne Meye Thompson puts it:

> As a church, it must draw the lines that exclude teaching and
> practise it deems out of harmony with the revelation of the
> Scripture. It has this right and responsibility. To be sure, in an
> effort to guard truth with zeal, some churches draw the lines
> too soon and too narrowly. But in the effort to exhibit
> Christian charity and tolerance, some churches refuse to draw
> the line at all. The continuing challenge to the church is to
> 'speak the truth in love'.[2]

Evangelicals stress that their fundamental commitments focus
around the two key doctrines of Scripture and the atonement.
Adopting such a position inevitably sets evangelicals apart from
others within the Christian community. David Edwards, in his
'liberal–evangelical dialogue' with John Stott, felt that the
evangelical insistence on such fundamentals was a handicap in
the communication of the gospel in the contemporary world:

> I long to persuade conservative Evangelicals that if only they
> can regard these ideas as optional (not necessarily wrong) they

will find that they can communicate the biblical gospel in terms which are far more intelligible, meaningful and credible.[3]

Stott was later to reply:

What worries me is your biblical selectivity. In later chapters you reject traditional teaching about the atonement, miracles, homosexual partnerships, and the awful reality of hell, not on the ground that you consider it unbiblical, but because on other grounds you find it unacceptable. Does this not mean that in the end you accord supremacy to your reason rather than to Scripture? We are back in the conflict between the Reformation and the Renaissance. As Luther said to Erasmus, 'The difference between you and me, Erasmus, is that you sit above Scripture and judge it, while I sit under Scripture and let it judge me!'[4]

Evangelical Christians, however, frequently make the mistake of imagining that they are the only Christians in the world. It is this which has sometimes given them an unfortunate reputation for arrogance. We should rejoice that all who profess Jesus Christ as Saviour, Lord and God share the name 'Christian'. There will be many differences between such Christians, at the level of both belief and practice. They might be Catholic, Orthodox or Protestant, but if they identify themselves as Christ's men and women, by both word and deed, then this will have important implications for the *manner* in which we might disagree.

There is also a balance expressed in the twofold aphorism which appears in Jesus' teaching recorded by Luke. 'Whoever is not against you is for you' (Lk. 9:50); and 'He who is not with me is against me' (Lk. 11:23). First, we should not discourage any activity which appears to be aiding God's work; secondly, those who are not clearly following the Lord as his disciples are to that extent hindering his work. Making such distinctions is not easy. It demands humility, and will come only through prayer, the study of Scripture, a proper understanding of the views of others, and corporate wisdom.

Whether we are evangelical or not, there are several levels of co-operation to be explored. Partnership among Christians will take different forms at each level. In many cases, joining hands with fellow believers will result in expanding opportunities for the cause of Christ and an enrichment in our fellowship and personal growth. In other cases, we shall conclude that partnership is not possible. In all cases, we need to demonstrate love for God's family members in a way which is consistent with the teaching we have explored.

Communication

At the most basic level, maintaining polite and open contact with churches and Christians of other persuasions is essential. For one thing, such association might lead to the dismantling of some of our traditional and inaccurate stereotypes. The kind of contact that is ready to get rid of false images that we hold of one another is obviously desirable all round. Some non-evangelicals are guilty of caricaturing evangelicals as uninterested in the scholarly study of Scripture, simplistic in their literal application of its truth, and certainly not interested in social or political issues. Among evangelicals, the same danger exists: we make our judgments of one another without clearly understanding who we are and what we stand for. I was once described by a church where I was invited to preach as 'charismatic'; I later discovered that they had applied this term because I had used an overhead projector! Equally, evangelicals are in danger of caricaturing liberals as those who hang loose to objective doctrinal truth, and therefore whose spirituality is suspect at every turn.

To be the victim of half-informed stereotypes is a painful experience, and is not something we should inflict on anyone, least of all those who share the name 'Christian'. In addition to understanding others more fully, we might well in turn come to see ourselves and our own commitments in a new light. John Stott's address, delivered at the International Congress on World Evangelization in Lausanne in 1974, was condemned by a few but accepted by the congress as a whole:

I do not propose to put up a few ecumenical skittles in order to knock them down with well-aimed evangelical balls, so that we can all applaud our easy victory! . . . I hope in my paper to strike a note of evangelical repentance . . . We have some important lessons to learn from our ecumenical critics. Some of their rejection of our position is not a repudiation of biblical truth, but rather of our evangelical caricatures of it.[5]

Communication will also mean simple courtesies. At the level of a local church, for example, if we are planning a children's holiday programme, an open-air service in the park, or a programme of literature distribution, it is common sense to inform other churches of our intentions. It is important in any community, whether a town or a university campus, to ensure that our actions are not in conflict. Similarly, if an evangelical student group is planning a mission in the college, courtesy demands that we inform others who are involved in Christian activity on the campus, whether denominational groups, chaplains or other Christian agencies.

Very often this also makes good sense from a pastoral perspective as far as churches are concerned. In my own experience as a church leader, it has not been unusual for people to move between one church and another in the city. If we find that certain people genuinely wish to transfer their membership from another church to our own (or *vice versa*), contact with the leadership of that church is not only a simple courtesy but may also be necessary from a pastoral or even disciplinary point of view. We all gain by talking together, and although this might not appear a particularly profound point to make, it is surprising how little our churches engage in such dialogue. Learning to listen, understand and communicate are the first essential steps all Christians should be ready to undertake.

Joint action

At a second level, we should also be ready to consider co-operation in certain specific areas of public life. Holding a different theological position as an evangelical should not necessarily close this option.

For example, there may well be areas of Christian compassion and social justice where joint statements and, even better, joint action, may be entirely appropriate. Not infrequently Christians must make a stand for certain moral values within their community, or work together in schemes designed to help those with housing or debt problems, or make representation to local authorities.

As evangelicals come to understand their heritage, they realize that many of their predecessors were committed to exactly this kind of social action and reform. Their belief in the authority and relevance of the gospel demanded that they should be ready to act in society in a way consistent with their firmly held beliefs. This is not the place for a full treatment of why evangelism and social action should be held together, but evangelical commitment to both of these has a long history. Our view of truth and love requires us to take seriously the body, the soul and the community. We have seen how truth leads to action, and how love demands obedience and practical care.

Some churches and Christian groups might conclude that such action is best left to individual members rather than being officially adopted by the community as a whole. A variety of reasons lie behind such a decision. For one thing, it is not always easy to determine a social or political action around which every member of the church can readily unite. But even if such unity of purpose exists, it is sometimes felt by evangelicals that co-operation on a social or political level with a group which adopts a very different doctrinal position might lead to misunderstanding. Might people assume that the church largely approves of the basic stance of the other group with which it is co-operating?

In my view, there are ways of minimizing this sort of misunderstanding. Occasions arise where a Christian Union, for example, can legitimately take a stand with others on certain issues (such as opposition to the paedophile movement). It can, if it wishes, make clear the limited nature of that co-operation or agreement, and this should be done in a sensitive manner. But in most cases this will not be necessary. The fact that Christians –

and even other religious groups within the community – wish to affirm their belief in the dignity and worth of human life, and act together in some way to express that conviction, will be understood by most thinking people. They will not usually jump to the conclusion that such groups therefore hold everything else in common.

Where corporate action is envisaged, the church or Christian student group will need to help its members understand the reasons for, and the limits of, such engagement with other groups. The issue will need to command their support and not be driven by the personal moral or political views of leaders alone. Clearly, the engagement of the whole group needs to be informed and, for a church or student group to be involved corporately, a proper sense of ownership and solidarity is required.

It is for some of these reasons that individual (rather than church) involvement is often seen as the most appropriate level for joint action of this kind. This should not mean that Christians are more passive than others about matters in their community which require action; as I have implied, our evangelical heritage has included substantial action and reform in areas of social and political concern. But we need to mobilize individuals who can, in good conscience, pursue the matter with other Christians or with other religious groups. This retains commitment to appropriate causes, while at the same time it avoids giving misleading impressions outside the church or Christian Union concerning what such joint action represents.

Evangelism

The painful dilemma for evangelical believers arises, however, over the issue of evangelizing with others. Since such common witness necessitates common faith, and co-operative evangelism demands agreement on the content of the evangel, it becomes necessary – indeed essential – to look hard at what we are being asked to do. It is a matter of fundamental integrity, as we have seen from John's uncompromising guidance in his second letter.

I would want to stress the fundamental importance of our working hard at every opportunity for partnership and co-operation which is consistent with the essentials of the gospel as we have defined them. We have already examined Jesus' prayer for the unity of God's people (chapter 6), and seen that it has special relevance to the church's mission. Jesus prayed for unity 'in order that' the world would believe. It is basic to the integrity and effectiveness of our evangelistic task. In the light of Jesus' prayer we must surely make every effort to find ways of working together with those who are committed to the gospel of Christ. Bruce Milne puts the case forcefully:

> Where the Holy Spirit has created the common life of the body of Christ among us, and agreement on the fundamentals of the revelation given through Jesus is present, it is unthinkable to pursue the mission of Jesus in isolation from, or even in competition with, those who are as truly the beloved objects of Jesus' prayer as we are.[6]

I began the present chapter by referring to the enormous need in Europe. We face the challenge of bringing the gospel once again to the continent's pagan millions. We cannot afford to do this as isolated churches or Christian organizations, and there are encouraging signs of growing partnership among evangelicals country by country as well as across the continent as a whole. Our limited experience in IFES is that, as students gain the vision for working together for Christ, they are able to join hands despite their differing denominational backgrounds because of their shared commitment to the foundation truths of the gospel. They learn to live with differences of a secondary nature and they remain solidly committed to their various churches. But they are able to see the gospel advance more effectively in their universities as a result of their partnership for that specific aim.

At the same time, our study of John 17 indicated that a straightforward appeal that we should co-operate 'as a demonstration of unity' needs to be unpacked. We have seen that unity arises from the nature of the gospel itself. The truth is personified in Jesus and in turn, he commissions us to bear witness to that truth in the world. The truth unites us and gives us a common purpose.

Consequently, where the truth is distorted, and the biblical message loses its force and power through deviations of one form or another, we cannot seek to co-operate in the hope that, by so doing, we shall work towards unity or somehow purify the message. Some of the strongest words in the New Testament concern those who preach a gospel at variance with the true apostolic message. Paul was passionate in his warnings to the churches:

> Even from your own number men will arise and distort the truth in order to draw away disciples after them. So be on your guard! Remember that for three years I never stopped warning each of you night and day with tears. *(Acts 20:30–31)*

He repeats this warning in his letter to the Galatians, with even more force:

> But even if we or an angel from heaven should preach a gospel other than the one we preached to you, let him be eternally condemned! As we have already said, so now I say again: If anybody is preaching to you a gospel other than what you accepted, let him be eternally condemned! *(Gal. 1:8–9)*

To the Thessalonians Paul had much the same to say, qualifying his remarks with an important pastoral observation, as we saw in the last chapter:

> If anyone does not obey our instruction in this letter, take special note of him. Do not associate with him, in order that he may feel ashamed. Yet do not regard him as an enemy, but warn him as a brother. *(2 Thes. 3:14–15)*

This sober emphasis of the New Testament demands that we view the matter of fundamental truth seriously. We cannot weaken or ignore what God has revealed in Scripture as the foundation of the gospel, however intolerant this may appear to others. Alongside the warning passages, there is also a positive emphasis on the importance of good teaching, particularly in

Paul's letters to Timothy (1 Tim. 4:6, 16; 2 Tim. 2:1–15; 3:15 – 4:7).

Our first duty, then, is clear. We are responsible to the God who has spoken, and to his revealed truth. His mercy in saving lost men and women cost him everything. We cannot compromise these gospel priorities for the sake of friendly relations. Gospel clarity is at the heart of our decision-making, for only then can we be faithful both to God and to the world that so desperately needs that message. To imagine that we are being more loving by being less demanding in this area is a dreadful travesty of God's loving heart and purpose for this world. Love requires us to uphold the gospel at all costs.

We have already stressed that the manner in which we defend and proclaim the truth is also critical. There is no room for harshness or pride. They are ugly characteristics in all relationships, and especially so when demonstrated by those who claim to uphold God's truth. Providing pastoral advice to one leader, Paul wrote:

> The Lord's servant must not quarrel; instead, he must be kind to everyone, able to teach, not resentful. Those who oppose him he must gently instruct, in the hope that God will grant them repentance leading them to a knowledge of the truth.
>
> *(2 Tim. 2:24–25)*

Love, Paul wrote, 'thinketh no evil' (1 Cor. 13:5, AV). This is the opposite of a censorious spirit. Too often we Christians display a spirit of malice, with its snap judgments and its perverse pleasure in finding fault. It appears to enjoy the negative attack on other people, except that it wears no smile. It has a conceited and arrogant disposition. It is conviction and judgment without love. For several years I edited a Christian magazine and, like most Christian writers and speakers, I received my share of hate mail. It should not have been a surprise, but not infrequently I felt a little sick at breakfast time as I read a blistering letter. Such a style of communication among Christians is not only distasteful; it dishonours the Lord to whom we each belong. We need to repent if our attitude and actions towards other Christians have displayed these unloving characteristics.

Nevertheless, there are times when, with humility and compassion, we must indicate that partnership is impossible with those who do not stand by the gospel as expressed clearly in the New Testament and as affirmed in the historic creeds of the church. James Denney, commenting on Paul's anathema in Galatians 1:8 (quoted above), expressed it in this way:

> The first commandment is 'Thou shalt have no other gods beside me' and that is the foundation of true religion. As there is only one God, so there can only be one Gospel. If God has really done something in Christ on which the salvation of the world depends, and if He has made it known, then it is a Christian duty to be intolerant of everything which ignores, denies or explains it away.[7]

An essential element of Christianity, therefore, is an intolerance of error. Our love for fellow believers is not expressed by an uncritical acceptance of all that they say, including what we would judge to be error. We shall develop a far stronger relationship, one of integrity and honesty, if we are prepared to face up to those differences (as we have seen in the previous chapter).

Primary and secondary

At the same time, we have seen that the New Testament speaks a great deal about another danger: the sin of schism. To cause trouble in the church is a serious matter with grave consequences. Paul warns that those who are guilty of selfish ambition, dissension and causing factions 'will not inherit the kingdom of God' (Gal. 5:20–21). Divisive Christians, according to the New Testament, are to be warned and then, if need be, excluded from fellowship (Tit. 3:9–10; Rom. 16:17).

Several passages of Scripture imply that a denial of certain doctrines is sufficient ground for withdrawing from people who regard themselves as Christians. Clearly, this has to do with the foundations of the faith, such as the denial of Christ's humanity or deity (1 Jn. 4:1–3) and the proclamation of 'another gospel' referred to in Galatians. Paul made some distinction between various doctrines. For instance, he plainly indicated that some matters are 'of first importance' (1 Cor. 15:3), and he was happy that Christ was being preached, even by members of the circumcision party (Phil. 1:15–18). In the last chapter we discussed the distinction between central and peripheral, primary and secondary. Similarly, the question of fellowship and co-operation hinges around the one issue: are the fundamentals of the gospel at stake?

Hard thinking

The net result of taking such teaching seriously is very practical. When considering co-operative activity in evangelism, a church and its leadership, or a college Christian Union, will need to work through some important questions.

First, do all the parties concerned believe the same things as fundamental to our faith and witness? The answer to this question will influence our decision with regard to the preaching and the preacher, the counsellors, the follow-up material and the churches to which converts are referred. When the gospel itself is at stake, we dare not compromise. If we conclude that we cannot co-operate, however, our hard work is not over. For, secondly, Christian love demands that we consider the way in which we may disagree, and the manner of any separation that may be necessary. 'The problem', says church historian Martin Marty, 'is that the civil people are not committed and the committed people aren't civil.'[8] A little overstated, but the point is clear. Evangelicals must at times take their stand for the purity of the gospel when it is not popular to do so. But there is no room for triumphalist slogans, proud thoughts, or words without actions. Such a stand, made with humility, is the only course which honours the tenor of Scripture in its appeal for faithfulness to the apostolic message.

I am all too aware of the difficulty of combining tough minds with tender hearts. In chapter 3 we saw how the mood of our culture, with its all-embracing inclusiveness, makes it hard for Christians to argue for the exclusive claims of the gospel. 'Any stigma is good enough to beat a dogma with.' Over against the spirit of the age, John's letters demonstrate that truth and love are not irreconcilable imperatives. As R. E. O. White comments:

> If 1 John leaves no shred of doubt that the attitude which glories in division, in the exclusive self-preserving separation, the self-congratulatory isolation which sets us apart from our brethren, is wholly deplorable and condemned, it leaves as little doubt that the sacrifice of Christian truth for the sake of conformity or compromise is equally deplorable, and as sharply condemned.[9]

The gospel defines our co-operation both in excluding those who reject it and in including those who affirm it. All around the world we face the urgent priority of strengthening partnership between all those who are Bible people and gospel people. A dying world needs to see the living church display the reconciling power of the gospel.

In summary, I offer a series of simple conclusions which I hope might help us to act with integrity and grace, conviction and compassion, as we consider ways of exercising Christian partnership.

Repent. Since Christ gave himself to reconcile us to God and to one another, we should mourn our divisions, and seek God's forgiveness for attitudes of pride, arrogance and malice. We should weep over, rather than rejoice in, the separation and intolerance which a commitment to the gospel sometimes requires.

Respect. Our contact with all other Christians, of whatever persuasion, should be characterized by courtesy, honesty and integrity. We should seek to listen as well as to witness clearly to the truth of the gospel as we perceive it.

Understand. We should reject all stereotypes of other Christian groupings, resist an unthinking rejection of all that they stand for, and seek to understand their position more clearly. This will also mean that, when called upon to describe their position, we should do so with accuracy. It will mean that we cannot keep our distance from those who do not believe as we do. When 'our only contact is to write books and articles against one another,' observes John Stott, 'grotesque caricatures develop in our imagination, until we can distinctly see in the other's profile the shape of horns, hooves and a tail'.[10]

Defend. We should not be ashamed to assert our conviction that the gospel is the heart of the matter. Today there is a discernible drift away from a central commitment to the cross: not that the atonement is denied, but that it is not the focal point of Christian proclamation. To fail to stand for the priorities of the gospel is to deny our first and most urgent duty to the God who saves and to the world which is lost.

Learn. We should be ready to receive from others what is genuinely of God, with gratitude and with humility. As those who seek to live under the authority of Scripture, we need to be ready to learn more of God's truth and love 'together with all the saints' (Eph. 3:18).

Engage. We should work at every opportunity for partnership with others, as far as is consistent with the gospel, with renewed energy and enthusiasm. Our concern for the church's unity must be as passionate as for its purity.

Discern. We should display an ability to enjoy true fellowship even while we disagree in those matters where Christians can disagree, following the lead given by Paul in urging loyalty to apostolic truth and liberty of conscience in secondary matters.

Act. We should refuse to compromise over those truths which are fundamental to the Christian gospel. When called upon to take a stand, we should be 'reluctant schismatics', like the sixteenth-century Reformers. When for truth's sake our conscience calls upon us to withdraw, we should not be afraid to do so – but with humility and regret, and no trace of self-righteousness.

Live. We should help one another to understand, communicate and live the foundation truths of biblical faith, demonstrating our passion for both truth and love through lives committed to holiness. We should give practical evidence that our Christian calling is not only to proclaim the faith of the gospel, but also to live lives worthy of it.

Notes

1. Murray Watts, *Bats in the Belfry* (Minstrel, 1989), p. 15.
2. Marianne Meye Thompson, *1–3 John*, IVP New Testament Commentaries (IVP, 1992), p. 156.
3. David L. Edwards and John Stott, *Essentials* (Hodder and Stoughton, 1988), p. 31.
4. *Ibid.*, pp. 104–105.
5. John Stott, 'The Biblical Basis of Evangelism', in J. D. Douglas (ed.), *Let the Earth Hear His Voice* (World Wide Publications, 1975), p. 65.
6. Bruce Milne, *The Message of John*, The Bible Speaks Today (IVP, 1993), p. 249.
7. James Denney, *The Death of Christ* (Tyndale, 1951), p. 103.
8. Quoted in Michael Kinnamon, *Truth and Community* (Eerdmans/WCC, 1988), p. 7.
9. R. E. O. White, *An Open Letter to Evangelicals* (Paternoster, 1964), p. 192.
10. John Stott, 'I Believe in the Church of England', in Gavin Reid (ed.), *Hope for the Church of England* (Kingsway, 1986), p. 29.

Christian growth

The city where I live has a population of 120,000, but over one million tourists visit us each year. Like other tourist cities, we have a love-hate relationship with them. They are a valuable source of income and their presence boosts local employment. But there is a cost. The traffic is terrible. Chattering hoards disturb the peace and clutter the pavements; Coke cans and McDonalds boxes litter the streets. And then there is the tourist 'mentality', the irritating tendency of people who have spent two hours touring the city on an open-top bus to declare: 'We've done Oxford.' They glide along in their air-conditioned coaches, they stay in the nice hotels, and after a brief expenditure of effort and mild perspiration, that's it: everything important has been done or seen.

The New Testament describes the Christian life not in terms of tourism but of pilgrimage. For the tourist, everything is immediate; for the pilgrim, it is long term. For the tourist, everything is quick, efficient and comfortable; for the pilgrim, it is a matter of hard work and steady perseverance towards the goal. Alongside the challenge of Christian beginning, the New Testament writers constantly emphasize Christian continuing. If you put your hand to the plough, you must press forward. If you have entered the marathon, you must keep running the race. If you have received Christ, you must grow up into his likeness.

Whether for the individual disciple or for a Christian congregation, the apostles encourage us to grow towards maturity. Paul mixes his metaphors as he insists that the building is to grow, the body is to be built up. What kind of Christian growth did he have in mind? What are the goals of our pilgrimage for which the apostles prayed and to which they gave their energies?

Many of Paul's prayers for young churches reflect his concern for progress towards maturity, and he frequently targets particular areas of growth. They include the twin themes of this book: truth and love. For the Philippians Paul prays 'that your love may abound more and more in knowledge and depth of insight' (1:9). The same clustering is found in his prayer of thanksgiving for the Colossians: 'We always thank God . . . when we pray for you, because we have heard of your faith in Christ Jesus and of the love you have for all the saints – the faith and love that spring from the hope that is stored up for you in heaven and that you have already heard about in the word of truth' (1:3–5). Perhaps the best-known couplet comes from Peter's concluding exhortation: 'Grow in the grace and knowledge of our Lord and Saviour Jesus Christ' (2 Pet. 3:18).

The apostles were clearly concerned to see Christians – indeed, whole congregations – enriching their lives and their service by a passionate commitment to a growing knowledge of the truth and a deepening experience of God's grace and love. It was this that brought maturity. Growing in grace and in knowledge would result in Christians becoming like Christ. And this is the essence of God's purpose in the gospel: to restore the family likeness, so that once again the human self and the Christian community come to reflect fully the image of God in Christ.

Throughout this book we have been stressing the integration of conviction and compassion, mind and heart. Christians have frequently polarized between 'a sharp mind and a warm heart', as Os Guinness puts it.[1] They have not always seen that the Spirit of truth is also the Spirit of love. But the apostles plainly urge upon us a growth towards all-round maturity, a commitment to grace and knowledge which will make us fully human as well as fully Christlike.

In drawing this book to a close, therefore, let me summarize four challenges to Christian growth where this balance of truth and love must be expressed.

A lively spirituality

Growing in grace and in knowledge is fundamental to a healthy spirituality. For some Christians, developing the spiritual life has been seen in cold, clinical terms. It has been reduced to a rather cerebral approach, almost to gathering information from the biblical text, with low expectations of engagement in any other area of the personality. In reaction, some Christians have understood spiritual development in anti-intellectual terms. It has become more mystical, more interiorized and meditative, and less content-full.

Christian maturity means growth in a rounded spirituality which embraces our spirits and minds, our wills and emotions, our imaginations and feelings. It involves everything about us, since we are growing in the knowledge of our Lord and Saviour, as Peter stressed (2 Pet. 3:18), and Christ's lordship should encompass every aspect of our humanity. Such growth in knowledge means far more than accumulating facts about Christ. It means a growth in relationship. Certainly, it will mean an increased awareness of gospel truth, since the context of Peter's exhortation to spiritual growth is one of warning; the previous verse urges believers to keep alert to the dangers of false teachers (2 Pet. 3:17). The same must be said of Paul's emphasis in Philippians 1:9; growth in love and knowledge certainly means to grow in our grasp of the truth, in its breadth and depth. But in both references it also means a deepening fellowship with him who is the Truth, whose love is poured out in our hearts by the Spirit.

It is this combination which seems to me to be so central to a lively spirituality. We are to feed our souls on the truth of God's Word and, as we believe and appropriate all that he has promised, so we receive his grace. Perhaps the greatest aspect of the Spirit's ministry towards us is not the spectacular or miraculous gifts which might immediately gain the attention of a spiritually hungry Christian, but his ministry of leading us deeper and deeper into a knowledge of the love of God in Christ. Consider another of Paul's prayers for growth:

> I pray that out of his glorious riches he may strengthen you with power through his Spirit in your inner being, so that Christ may dwell in your hearts by faith. And I pray that you, being rooted and established in love, may have power, together with all the saints, to grasp how wide and long and high and deep is the love of Christ, and to know this love that surpasses knowledge – that you may be filled to the measure of all the fulness of God.
> (Eph. 3:16–19)

Paul uses three simple pictures here to emphasize his desire that we should grow towards this kind of maturity. First, *dwelling*. Why does he pray that Christ should dwell in their hearts when they are already believers? The word he chooses speaks of feeling at home, of belonging there. He longs that Christ would settle down in their hearts and lives. Secondly, he prays that they may be *rooted*. The picture is agricultural, and again stresses depth, not superficiality. Their source of nourishment and stability as Christians will be God's love. His third picture, of being *grounded*, is an architectural term; Paul is reminding them of their foundations. They are building their lives solidly on the rock of God's love. They have deep roots and firm foundations; God's love provides them with all they need.

Paul links this experience of love with their understanding. Their knowledge does not come about simply through reading, studying and accumulating information. It comes as they grasp the vastness of God's love. Here is the paradox of Paul's words: we are to know the love of Christ 'that surpasses knowledge'. Christ's riches are unsearchable, and his love is beyond our understanding, but we are to apply our hearts and minds in experiencing this overwhelming vastness.

This is the place of spiritual life and growth, the beginning of revival. It is all too easy for evangelical spiritual life to be driven by an unhealthy activism which can produce guilt trips, burnout, and what Alister McGrath calls 'more than its fair share of walking wounded'.[2] But spiritual vitality begins with reflecting regularly on 'how great is the love the Father has lavished on us' (1 Jn. 3:1). Knowing that we are the loved children of God is at the heart of our true identity as believers. Experiencing his accepting, healing, nurturing love can motivate us day by day to become what we are and what we should be.

Commenting on 1 John 3, David Jackman writes:

> There are many Christians who cannot really accept this lavish love of God for them personally. They are always trying to be good enough to persuade God to love them, rather than accepting the fact that he already does. So they embark on a ceaseless treadmill of Christian activity, always trying to prove to themselves and others that their grades are good enough to pass with God . . . Security comes through realizing that our identity as God's dearly loved children depends not on our activity, but on his electing grace.[3]

Perhaps the neatest way of expressing what a lively spirituality means is found in a proverb which unites our twin themes. Using the same two words that we examined in chapter 2, the teacher urges us:

> Let love and faithfulness never leave you;
>   bind them around your neck,
>   write them on the tablet of your heart.

(Pr. 3:3)

He uses strong expressions to underline that these qualities should be deeply ingrained within us; not only are we to meditate upon them, but they should be so much a part of us that they naturally express themselves in all that we are, say and do. Love and truth are to be fully integrated into our lives. They are to be written on our hearts and minds, part of who we are and shaping all of our responses.

When God's steadfast love and faithfulness are penetrating our lives in this way, the result is a lively spirituality that is strongly attractive because it is profoundly Christlike.

A genuine integrity

'The curse of today', writes George Verwer, 'is orthodoxy without love, orthodoxy without power, orthodoxy without the life of our Lord Jesus Christ.'[4] Religion without life is repellent to today's generation. It is hollow and irrelevant. It says nothing to a world of need. Throughout this book we have underlined that the Christian gospel reflects God's concern for transformed lives, for truth embodied and for love demonstrated. Just as knowing and experiencing these qualities lie at the heart of a lively spirituality, so they are essential if our Christian service is to have integrity.

Today we are facing a crisis of 'models'. We are frequently told that we are in need of moral leadership but that there are few who can provide it. Young people look for role models but conclude that there are none. Yet one impressive feature of Paul's ministry was his *example*. The gospel advanced with a ripple effect, as a direct result of the impact of lives lived with integrity. We can trace this process in 1 Thessalonians: 'you know how we lived among you' (1:4); 'you became imitators of us and of the Lord' (1:6); 'you became a model to all the believers' (1:7); 'you . . . became imitators of God's churches in Judea' (2:14).

Paul's life demonstrated the truth and power of the gospel. Indeed, he stresses that the gospel advanced not by proclamation alone. 'Our gospel came to you not simply with words, but also with power, with the Holy Spirit and with deep conviction' (1:5). 'We loved you so much that we were delighted to share with you not only the gospel of God but our lives as well, because you had become so dear to us' (2:8).

His ministry involved nurturing his fellow believers, and this led to a relational intensity that is expressed in very affectionate terms. 'We were gentle among you, like a mother caring for her little children' (2:7); 'We loved you so much' (2:8); 'we dealt with each of you as a father deals with his own children' (2:11).

Christian ministry is driven by a sense that the gospel is true (it is the word *of God*, 2:13; Paul is very emphatic) coupled with an experience of the love and grace of God who has called us ('brothers loved by God', 1:4). The consequence is a life entirely devoted to others, a life of such integrity that its witness to Christ ripples out, wave after wave, as more and more lives are impacted by its power.

It is this genuine integrity that our friends and neighbours need to see. We must preach, but we must also demonstrate. We cannot be like the teacher, whose presentation of the message in the lecture theatre is immaculate but whose life has no bearing on the validity of what he says. Consistent Christianity is the only credible Christianity. It is a witness to the gospel of truth lived out in radical obedience. Integrity in our lives demands truth worked out in action, love expressed in obedience.

A dynamic community

As we have seen, one of the most rigorous testing-grounds for Christians lies in their relationships with fellow believers. If the Christian community cannot give practical evidence of true reconciliation, it casts doubt on the reality and power of the gospel of reconciliation. This is why Jesus prayed so fervently that the disciples would be truly one, 'so that the world may believe' (Jn. 17:21).

We have stressed that truth and love belong together in our congregations. Earlier we referred to Paul's prayer for the Ephesians, in which he longed that they would know and experience God's love 'together with all the saints' (3:18). So too, in his image of growth and maturity in Ephesians 4, Paul expresses his concern that there should be corporate growth in truth and love. The goal is that the body of Christ will be built up 'until we all reach unity in the faith and in the knowledge of the Son of God and become mature' (verse 13). It is a growth towards unity in truth. And how is that maturity to be achieved? 'From him the whole body, joined and held together by every supporting ligament, grows and *builds itself up in love*, as each part does its work' (verse 16).

The imagery here implies that something dynamic is going on within the congregation. The important combination is once again expressed in verse 15: 'speaking the truth in love'. Paul's verb here embraces not only speaking but also being and doing; he is talking about living the truth in an environment of love.

The church is on the move; it is heading somewhere. God's building project is steadily being completed 'as each part does its work'.

This, then, is a further challenge to our Christian witness. Our congregations must be dynamic communities of change as we grow together in mature understanding and as we develop relationally. It will mean a far greater personal vulnerability than we are sometimes used to, and a demanding commitment of time and effort if we are to build up Christian community in a way that demonstrates these profound qualities.

A deepening intensity

Much modern Christianity is pale and bland. It has no cutting edge, no fire, no passion. As Roy Clements once observed,

> People used to talk about the church 'militant', but we have abdicated that word to the left-wing politicians. The average church member today is more emotionally involved in his football team than in the kingdom of God. He or she is more moved by the latest soap opera than by the gospel of Christ.

Peter was of a temperament that naturally went to extremes. Whether in betrayal or in devotion, he did not do things by halves. He was not one of the men in grey suits. His letters adopted the same tone. When writing about the Christian life he anticipated wholehearted commitment on the part of his readers. In his first letter he was deeply concerned that Christians should live differently as a result of their new life in Christ. They should experience the full growth of this new life with a fervour and passion worthy of the gospel.

Christians, says Peter, are to be characterized by obedience to the truth and by love for each other. Their response to the truth is complete submission and obedience (1 Pet. 1:2, 14, 22). It was this submission to 'the living and enduring word of God' that had brought about their new life (1:22–23). In turn, that complete commitment to the truth meant a fervent devotion towards others. 'Now that you have purified yourselves by obeying the truth so that you have sincere love for your brothers, love one another deeply, from the heart' (1:22). The word translated 'deeply' really means 'with full intensity' or 'at full stretch'. Be wholehearted. Give everything in your response. Paul expresses the same intensity: 'I long for all of you with the affection of Christ Jesus' (Phil. 1:8).

There is little doubt in my mind that if we Christians are to have any chance at all of making a serious impact in our time, we must rediscover a passion for these two elements: being faithful to the commands of Jesus, and demonstrating his love. We need to become fanatics for the truth and love that are found in him, our hearts and minds set on fire with a devotion to Christ, and our Christian service defined by a passion for people. Our mission as disciples and as churches is to live his life with an ever-deepening intensity. This is the New Testament vision of growth, culminating in the completion which we shall witness in heaven, 'attaining to the whole measure of the fulness of Christ' (Eph. 4:13).

The opening words of this book reminded us that Jesus' ministry to the woman caught in adultery was directed to making her whole, not to tearing her apart. His commitment to each of us is the same. This is why the Christian gospel is such good news for a fractured world.

It stands in contrast both to lifeless religion, with its impossible rules and its dry orthodoxy; and to the empty promises of materialism, the powerlessness of contemporary therapies, the confusion of New Age experience and the desperation and disorientation of a postmodern age. It offers a message of reconciliation, a profound re-creation which restores the image of God in Christ to each person, however broken, who turns to him in repentance and faith. It builds true community as individuals are bound together by the Word and the Spirit. It is a message of truth and love that is no mere ideology, but a life-transforming dynamic that is changing lives the world over. In short, Christianity is Christ, the Way, the Truth and the Life. There is no safer Guide in this universe, no greater Lover, and no-one worthier of our full commitment.

Notes

1. This theme is developed in Os Guinness, *Fit Bodies, Fat Minds* (Hodder and Stoughton, 1995), p. 31.
2. Alister McGrath, *The Future of Evangelicalism* (Hodder and Stoughton, 1994), p. 151.
3. David Jackman, *The Message of John's Letters*, The Bible Speaks Today (IVP, 1988), p. 83.
4. George Verwer, *A Revolution of Love and Balance* (STL, 1977), p. 14.

God's Good Life
The Ten Commandments for the 21st century
DAVID FIELD

Ever feel tempted to covet your neighbour's ox? Or make your maidservant work on the sabbath?

Come off it! The Ten Commandments were meant for ancient Israelites, not for sophisticated westerners with a foot in the door of the twenty-first century!

Or were they?

When you've finished reading this book you may well change your mind. Those ancient stone tablets have a great deal to say to us today after all! They are God's way in to the truly good life.

With questions for thought and discussion

David Field teaches ethics at Oak Hill Theological College, London, where he is Vice-Principal. He is married with three grown-up children.

240 pages   *Pocketbook*

Inter-Varsity Press

The Meanings of Love

ALAN STORKEY

The idea of love has millions of supporters. Each generation applauds it both loudly and in romantic whispers. Everyone wants to give it and to receive it. Yet every night men and women sob as they realize that for them love has died. And the cynics are getting younger.

What is love? Why do we so often get it wrong? Why do lovers experience – and cause – such hurt?

This book investigates the models of man–woman love which we often espouse, shows where they lead, and explores their inner logic. It encourages us to examine what is going on in our own relationships. It points us to the place where the true meaning of love is to be found, so that we can begin to prove its gentle power in our lives.

Alan Storkey lectures in sociology at Oak Hill College, London, and is a member of the Church of England Board of Social Responsibility's working party on 'The Future of the Family'. He is married to Elaine and they have three sons. His interests include painting, art history and chess.

176 pages   'B' format

INTER-VARSITY PRESS

The Message of Deuteronomy
Bible Speaks Today series
RAYMOND BROWN

Western society at the end of the second millenium AD is increasingly technological, highly sophisticated and largely urban. How then can a book concerned with the migration and settlement of a group of tribes in the second millenium BC be relevant to us today?

Raymond Brown shows how the timeless truths and universal principles in Deuteronomy provide a guiding pattern for the wide range of issues that confront us today – from business management to personal morality. The Lord who demanded allegiance then in all details of human life and society still claims authority over modern humanity.

No part of the Old Testament, Raymond Brown believes, has exerted a greater influence on the formation and development of both Jewish and Christian thought and lifestyle than Deuteronomy. Its continuing and dramatic relevance is opened up by his compelling exposition.

Dr Raymond Brown was formerly Principal of Spurgeon's College, London. He has also written on Hebrews for this series.

336 pages   *Large paperback*

Inter-Varsity Press